Redefining Work-Life Balance

One-Minute Tools to Manage Stress,
Achieve More & Enjoy Life Every Day

By
Jim Bird

ISBN: 9781948787833

For my wife, Vikki, and daughters, Amanda and Kelly.
You inspire me every day.

Contents

Introduction

As a star consultant in a major international firm, Mark had been on more flights in the last month than he could recall. He was exhausted at the thought of another trip. With the hypnotizing hum of the plane's engine in the background, he stared out the window at the oncoming dusk and thought, *If this plane would just crash, I wouldn't have to take on the additional responsibilities looming ahead of me.* For a moment, he considered that a positive.

That dreadfully shocking thought fundamentally changed the way Mark chose to balance his life for the better. He did not change his definition of professional success. Instead, he redefined his work-life balance to achieve it. Now, as the twenty-year president of a major US distribution company and a proud and happy husband and father, he says, "That was a tipping point that made me more productive *and* more fulfilled in my career and my personal life."

Redefining your work-life balance in the right way has life-altering results. These pages capture that better way for you to define your best work-life balance and are supported by radically simple yet powerful tools, many of which become enjoyable habits you will consistently apply in one minute or less.

The immediate outcomes you should expect are more fulfilling relationships with those you love and care about, more joy and less tension within yourself, and more pride, satisfaction, and accomplishment in your work and with your co-workers. Over a lifetime, the tools and concepts in these pages will reduce negative stress and create more positive balance in and between your work and personal life…every day.

I have been passionate about this topic since my senior year at Georgia Tech where I participated in an honors research project. I could choose any topic and for my efforts receive an automatic "A" grade. I jumped at the opportunity. I told my professor that I wanted to create a framework and tools for how to be very successful in business *and* enjoy life's journey along the way.

My professor resisted at first, saying it was too broad, but eventually he gave in. The result was one of the most important experiences of my life. It gave me the opportunity to research and study a wide range of subjects that I was interested in—leadership, ethics, people skills, philosophy, time management—and resulted in a very early framework and tool set.

The techniques developed from that research were tested and substantially modified in the real world. I started and grew a light manufacturing business to a great team of 300+ people generating over $100 million in sales. A big part of our team's commitment and success came from adapting and applying these tools and respecting that in addition to having a job, each one of us has a life.

I later built an international leadership and work-life balance training firm where those techniques were refined by working with Mark and hundreds of other outstanding leaders and organizations to create a more positively balanced and happier life. Along the way, I fell in love and added the experience of becoming a very proud and appreciative husband and dad.

The result of decades of learning from and teaching others are found in the practical tools contained in this book. These tools have proven to better balance and enhance people's lives in their work and in relationships with family and friends and their own personal well-being.

As part of that process I have personally asked tens of thousands of individuals in businesses, non-profits, government agencies, and the U.S. military whether work-life balance is an important issue to them and what results they would like to see by better achieving it. Overwhelmingly, it was an important issue and their most common desired benefits included:

- More fulfilled
- Less stressed

- More productive personally and professionally
- Get more important things done in less time
- Procrastinate less
- Stay focused amidst all the distractions
- Have time just for me
- Be happier

These are all results that the tools in our training and in this book produced for them and will for you, as well. However, before applying these tools to create a more positive work-life balance, we must first clearly *redefine* balance in a way that works for you.

Regrettably, that has become necessary because academics, HR departments, and the media have shallowly defined work-life balance in ways that make it unattainable, undesirable, or both. Too often these straw man definitions are used to conclude that work-life balance does not exist. "Work-Life Balance Is Dead" and "Work-Life Balance is Impossible" have been repeated headlines in hundreds of media pieces from Forbes, Fortune, and CNN amongst numerous others who grabbed a catchy title and ran with it.

If something you inherently desire is undefined, ill-defined, or "impossible," your outcomes will disappoint or frustrate and can often be harmful. Fortunately, these pundits are wrong. Work-life balance is attainable every day for the rest of your life, provided it is positively redefined from these self-defeating characterizations.

That's why Part One of this book begins by dispelling the myth that there is no such thing as work-life balance. Instead it delivers a proven re-definition that is clear, fulfilling, and attainable, along with a tool set that will enhance the value and positive balance you get from life—today and every day.

Part Two is about people and relationships. You will learn two powerful one-minute tools that can be applied to your life immediately. The outcome will be a more rewarding, less stressed, and happier balance with the important individuals in your personal and work life. In each chapter you will also see examples from people who have generously shared their personal stories and experiences in implementing these tools.

Part Three is about achieving the *things* you want in life. It delivers two tools that supercharge your thinking. You will get more quality thinking done with each of these tools in minutes than most people get done in days, weeks, or even a lifetime of typical pondering.

You will also discover two balance measurement tools: one gauges your emotional status and reactions and the other illuminates your current emphasis in life and enables you to easily adjust it, if it is not where you want it to be.

Part Four concludes these pages using your definition of optimal work-life balance to clarify your Way of Life goals. These goals are not specific markers to surpass or milestones to accomplish but *ways of living*. What are the most meaningful and important outcomes you want in life every day? You will be surprised how quickly these meaningful and often life-changing goals become clear with this final tool in the book.

My promise to you is that by applying these proven tools you will create immediate positive outcomes personally and professionally. More importantly, from feedback across demographics, countries, and cultures, I expect you will retain and use the tools you find most helpful along with a re-definition of work-life balance to be happier, less stressed, and more fulfilled over your lifetime.

Let's turn the page and redefine work-life balance in a way that works for you.

PART ONE

Redefining
Work-Life Balance

1

Work-Life Balance Redefined

"When shall we live if not now?"
Seneca

Despite the worldwide quest for Work-Life Balance, very few have found an acceptable definition of the concept. This lack of a clear and agreed upon definition has led some leaders to shun the term or claim that balance between work and life does not exist in the modern "always-on" world.

Most attempts that have been made to define it revolve around balancing time between hours at work and time spent in our personal lives with friends, family, and self. This may be well-intentioned, but it results in an ultimately failed definition and outcome. It's unrealistic to expect to spend equal time in all areas of your life or even remain consistent in how you proportion your time spent. With this flawed premise, it's no wonder we believe that work-life balance can't possibly exist!

Even great leaders have publicly spoken out against the concept. Take Jack Welch, the well-regarded business leader and former Charmain and CEO of General Electric, who said, "There is no such thing as work-life balance. There are work-life choices, and you make them, and they have consequences."[1]

I would challenge the notion that because work-life choices have consequences you cannot have balance. When work-life balance is defined in an attainable way, its very definition guides us to make better choices that result in a more meaningful and fulfilling balance.

We will not get to a positive work-life balance outcome until we define it in a way that is realistically attainable. First, we must dispel some misconceptions and define what work-life balance is NOT.

Work-life balance does not mean an equal balance of time spent. Work-life balance is not defined by *hours* but by *outcomes*. Trying to schedule an equal number of hours for each of your various work and personal activities is usually under-rewarding and unrealistic. Life is and should be more fluid than that.

Your best work-life balance choices will vary over time and circumstances, often on a daily basis. I expect your weekday priorities change from those on a weekend. In the long run, your work-life balance decisions will be different when you are single than if you choose to marry or have children; when you start a new career versus when you are nearing retirement.

There is no perfect, one-size fits all solution. The best work-life balance choices are different for each of us because we all have different priorities and different lives.

Because of this, the definition of work-life balance must get at the root of what motivates our lives yet be flexible and adaptable to individual priorities and life objectives. I have been studying this topic and working with some of the busiest executives in the world for decades and have found that at the core of an effective work-life balance definition are two key everyday concepts that are relevant to each of us. These two concepts deliver more meaning and balance in our everyday life and over an entire lifetime—they cost nothing and are attainable by

---

[1] Rachel Emma Silverman, "Jack Welch: 'No Such Thing as Work-Life Balance.'" *Wall Street Journal,* July 13, 2009.

anyone, regardless of income, age, or current circumstance. They are daily **Achievement and Enjoyment**, ideas almost deceptive in their simplicity.

Our Achievements and Enjoyments, big and small, create the meaningful and valued life we all seek. In many ways, Achievement and Enjoyment are the two most powerful and essential drivers of good in the world and in each of our lives. These two concepts answer the big question: "Why?" Why do you want a better income? A new house? To put the kids through college? To do a good job today? To come to work at all?

It is human nature to want and need both Achievement and Enjoyment. These two concepts represent the front and back sides of the coin of value in life. Imagine you are holding a one-ounce gold coin in your hand. It's valuable—depending on the current market, it's probably worth well over $1000. Now let's say you want a lot more of those coins, but for some reason you don't like the two-sided thing. You want one-sided coins. Is that possible?

No. If you try to have a one-sided coin, poof, the coin disappears; the value vanishes. The same is true in life. If you try and get the value of life just from the Achievement side or just from the Enjoyment side—poof—much of the value of life disappears. Living a one-sided life is why so many "successful" people are not happy, or not nearly as happy as they could be. The more we wrap our minds around these two principles and fold them into our daily lives, the more balance, productivity, and joy we will find.

Most of us already have a solid grasp on the meaning of Achievement. I expect you are working to make it happen and achieve things every day. But it's helpful to clarify the definition of *Enjoyment* in the context of how we live our life and set our goals. Enjoyment certainly means "Ha-Ha" happiness. Did you hear a good joke or have fun or a good laugh today? Enjoyment also means having a sense of pride, satisfaction, celebration, love, affection, well-being—all the joys of living.

For me, one of my greatest joys is fishing. As I'm writing this, I'm imagining I have a fishing rod in my hands. It's bent to 90 degrees, and the reel is screeching as a monster fish rips line from the spool. I literally have goose bumps right now just imagining the leaps, the catch, the release. I love fishing and the joy that connecting with nature brings me. What are your passionate joys? What stirs your heart or adds Enjoyment to your life?

The life-changing power of incorporating these two priorities, particularly Enjoyment, into your way of living every day is often overlooked because of its seeming simplicity. I have a business acquaintance who is a self-made billionaire. When I first met him after a CEO program I conducted in Boston, he was in his late sixties. I knew him as a pioneer in hardware technology and a wonderfully effective philanthropist. After the session he came up to me and said, "Jim, I always got this Achievement thing. But I never got the Enjoyment thing. I never had it as a conscious goal. It never was at the forefront of my mind. I just assumed that if I achieved, the Enjoyment would come. But it doesn't. I now realize that Enjoyment doesn't come any more automatically in life than Achievement does."

And he's right. When you are in high school or college, if you've got a date on Friday night, then everything's great. Enjoyment comes easy. But when you are thrust into the real world of work responsibilities, car payments, house payments, and relationship responsibilities, then Enjoyment does not happen any more automatically than Achievement. Like Achievement, to happen routinely, Enjoyment needs to be a conscious goal at the forefront of your mind; an important part of the purpose for your day.

The CEO added, "If I simply had made Enjoyment an everyday goal and focus, not only would I have enjoyed my life so much more, but I would have achieved even more." He saw where he had missed connecting with individuals and cultures to accomplish more because he seldom linked to the Enjoyment side of their work or life. He rarely paused to celebrate with them the joy, sense of fulfillment, and meaning in minor and major achievements that are important motivators for most of us to continue to excel.

I expect when you got up this morning you had Achievement goals for the day. Meetings at work, projects requiring your attention, getting the kids to school, or chores at home. What were your Enjoyment goals for the day? Did you have Enjoyment as a committed goal for the day?

If you want Enjoyment to be a consistent part of your balanced life, as it should be, you must firmly plant it in the forefront of your mind as an everyday expectation.

Avoiding the "As Soon As" Trap

Intentionally incorporating BOTH Achievement and Enjoyment into your daily way of living also helps you avoid the "As Soon As" Trap, the life-dulling habit of delaying accomplishments and the joys of life. Have you ever been caught in an "As Soon As" Trap? "As soon as we move out of this cramped little apartment, I'll be happy"; "As soon as I get the promotion, I can relax a little"; or "As soon as I finish this project at work honey, I'll talk to you more often again." I've heard people say, "As soon as I get married, life is going to be great," and sometimes it is. But sometimes, six or seven years later, the same folks are saying, "As soon as the divorce goes through, I can start living again." Life does not work that way. And if you are not careful, you can "as soon as" your entire life away.

My caffeine source is diet cola. However, I'm a somewhat fussy diet cola drinker. I don't like cans or bottles. I like fountain cola. And there is a big difference in the cola depending on the soda fountain. So, I know all the best fountains within a five-mile radius of my house and office. My favorite is a little convenience store near my home called Fitzgerald's.

Let's say I'm wandering into Fitzgerald's at 6:00 a.m. in my pre-caffeinated state. As I'm walking in, some guy bumps into me, looks up, and says, "Hey, mister, what's your purpose in life?"

Well, even in my foggy, half-awake condition, I'd have an answer for him, because it is very clear to me. I'd say: "I just want to **achieve** something today and I want to **enjoy** something today. And if I do both of those things today, I'm going to have a pretty good day. And if I do both of those things **every day**, for the rest of my life, I'm going to have a pretty good life."

And I think that is true for all of us. Life will deliver more of the value and positive balance we desire when we are achieving and enjoying something every single day in the important relationship areas that make up our lives: our work, our families, our friends and communities, and the relationships we have with ourselves.

As a result, we've found a good working definition of Work-Life Balance is:

**Meaningful, <u>daily</u> Achievement *and* Enjoyment
in each of the four life quadrants: Work, Family, Friends, and Self.**

Your specific objectives and time spent in each quadrant will vary, often by the day. So, when we use the term "quadrant," we mean four areas of life, not four time-equal areas. But whatever the time spent in each quadrant, meaningful achievement *and* enjoyment should be an everyday goal and expectation.

Achievement and Enjoyment are not either/or. You are not trading one off for the other. When positively fused together, they multiply each other and are powerfully life enhancing. At work, you can create your own best work-life balance by making sure you not only Achieve but also reflect the joy of the job, and the joy of life, **every day**. If nobody pats you on the back today, pat yourself on the back. And help others to do the same.

When you do, when you are a person that not only gets things done, but also enjoys the doing, it attracts people to you. They want you on their team and they want to be on your team. Simple concepts. Once you focus on them as key components of your day, they are not that hard to implement.

Ask yourself now, when was the last time you Achieved AND Enjoyed something at work? What about Achieved AND Enjoyed with your family, or your friends? And how recently have you Achieved AND Enjoyed something just for you? Consciously realizing both of these way-of-living goals *every day*, even in small ways, immediately changes your work-life balance for the better. Doing so consistently will multiply your achievements *and* enjoyments and create a happier, less stressed, and more fulfilling balance for you, your family, and all those important individuals you care about over a lifetime.

Summary

- Work-life balance is not defined by *hours* but by *outcomes*.
- Achievement and Enjoyment are the two most powerful and essential drivers of good in the world and in each of our lives.
- Therefore, a good working definition of work-life balance is: "Meaningful daily Achievement *and* Enjoyment in each quadrant of your life: Work, Family, Friends, and Self."
- Consciously incorporating both Achievement and Enjoyment into your daily way of living also helps you avoid the life-dulling "As Soon As" Trap.

2

The Choice Challenge

Why Work-Life Balance Is a Critical Skill for the Future

*"And in the end, it's not the years in your life that count.
It's the life in your years"*
— Abraham Lincoln

You probably start most days with a full plate. If you are working, you jump into a busy daily schedule with meetings, deadlines, and plenty of emails to address…and then someone calls an unplanned meeting. Leaving that meeting, your boss asks you take on some additional responsibility. Then, as you walk back to your desk, your phone is ringing. On top of it, you have received several urgent text messages. Later in the day, just when you think you have a handle on it all, a fire drill pops up. In addition to all of this, you have a personal life…or I hope you do.

Over the past five decades, our world has changed to make the daily Achievement and Enjoyment equation MUCH more challenging. Technology and modern conveniences have both enhanced our daily lives and added to the complexity of everyday living.

All of this can be challenging both personally and professionally. But is it really different from past generations? Based on research, the answer is a resounding: "Yes!" Our daily lives today are vastly different and more complex than those of past generations.

Take a look at the graph below.[2]

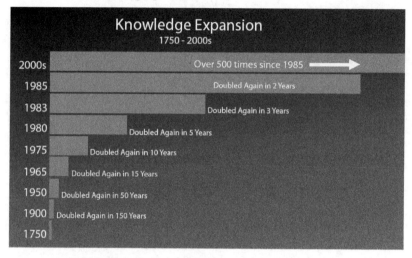

On a daily basis you are exposed to over 100 times as much information and knowledge as your parents were a generation ago; 400 times your grandparents.

What has caused this explosion of information? The biggest driver has been technological advancement: the internet, email, texting, tweets, blogs, smart phones, and social media. Before 1950 there was very little television. Until the 1990s, TV was dominated by only a few channels. Today there are more than 1000 television channels. Unquestionably much of this information is junk. But there has also been a great expansion of valuable knowledge that can benefit our jobs and personal lives.

What we often don't recognize is that along with this explosion of information comes an explosion of choices. Choices that we must make every day. This explosion of information and opportunities has led to the greatest "choice challenge" any generation has ever known.

---

[2]   R. Buckminster Fuller, "Knowledge Doubling Curve," *Critical Path*, 1982.

The typical way we look at these choices is, "How do I juggle all these balls?" Given that there are over one hundred times as many choices to make, we have gone from this

in the 1960s...   to this in the 80s...

to this where we are today.

Can you relate? Almost all of us in the developed and developing world can. In the future, our options will continue to expand at ever-increasing rates.

Most forward-looking individuals and organizations see the expanding torrent of choices as a blessing. We have the greatest opportunity ever to achieve a happy and fulfilling life.

But opportunity does not always mean results. Successfully prioritizing our work-life choices is both more difficult and more critical than ever before.

Robert Ornstein and Richard Thompson in their book *The Amazing Brain* put it this way: "The problem is that our ability to create always leaps ahead of our ability to adapt, and we are forever locked into a cycle of adapting to unprecedented situations."

Our challenge as individuals is to make sure we have a process to take advantage of all those choices and not be overwhelmed by them. Our responsibility as leaders is to make sure that the people we care about, the people we are responsible for, are also exposed to skills to manage and take advantage of this challenge.

How do we develop a simple process to train our brain to leap ahead in the human cycle of creating and adapting to this multitude of expanding opportunities?

The first step is to move away from the idea of juggling priorities altogether. Just look back at that juggler visual. It's confusing, frustrating, and very stressful. There's got to be a better way to wisely choose from our abundance of responsibilities and choices. And there is.

A Simpler Way – Your Life as a Puzzle

It begins by thinking of life as a *big puzzle* that never runs out of pieces. Rather than trying to keep everything in the air at once, think about your choices like puzzle pieces. You want to replace the whole idea of juggling with a simple way of sorting, selecting, and connecting the pieces you want to be part of your "Big Picture" and have a way to let the other pieces go.

Think for a moment about putting a puzzle together. What is the first thing you do when you start?

Usually it is some type of broad sort, such as finding the edges or the corners. Then you do a sub-sort...like finding the edges that are blue. And then you keep sorting down until you identify two pieces that fit together to make the picture look the way you want it to.

In our big picture there are four key areas that all our responsibilities, relationships, and decisions fall into. They serve us well as our first broad puzzle sort and they should come as no surprise. These four quadrants of your life are:

- Your Work
- Your Family
- Your Friends & Community and...
- Your Self

Your Big Picture

Friends & Community   **Self**

Family   **Work**

The whole idea of work-life balance has led many people to think of life as just "what happens at work" and everything else, but just sorting your life into "work" and "personal" is not enough. Your personal life has too many pieces and is far too complex to be in one big pile. Instead you will find it more useful to sort the components of your life into the four areas of Work, Family, Friends/Community, and Self.

After selecting a quadrant, the next critically important sort is to is to recognize that all of your goals and objectives in that quadrant are accomplished by managing primarily only one of two things. They are your relationships with *people* or the *projects* and related activities you undertake.

Think about this. If we manage all of our relationships, both business and personal ones, as well as we can, and we manage all of our projects and activities as well as we can, *what else is there to manage?* Not much.

What makes your puzzle come together well is *not how much time you spend* in each area. Rather, it is the quality of your relationships and the projects and activities you put in place to make your life puzzle look the way you want it to. The bulk of your life's memories, achievements and enjoyments come from these two things—people and projects. These are what make your puzzle "click" and enable you to achieve and enjoy life to its fullest.

This is why Part Two and Three of this book provide tools to help you nurture more successful relationships and projects. These tools allow you to quickly sort your most important people and projects in each quadrant of your life to make your Big Picture puzzle happier, less stressed, and more fulfilled.

But just sorting and deciding on your most important People and Project pieces is not enough to balance your life. You must also commit to them in a way that makes them happen; that connects each piece into its place in your real life. That's why we begin with WIN as Tool #1 in the next chapter. It will connect your people and project priorities to your life and insure you more consistently follow through to Achieve and Enjoy more every day.

Summary

- Successfully prioritizing your work-life choices is both more difficult and more crucial now than in prior generations.
- Instead of juggling life's priorities, think of life as a big puzzle, "Your Big Picture," with choices being pieces that need to be sorted and selected.
- Your Big Picture includes four key quadrants: Work, Family, Friends & Community, and Self.
- Sorting your responsibilities and relationships into these four quadrants is the first foundational step to better balance your life's choices.

3

The Commitment Tool

WIN® – Tool #1

"I work as hard as anyone,
And yet, I get so little done,
I'd do so much you'd be surprised,
If I could just get organized!"
— Douglas Malloch

To make your dreams, your passions, and your desired Achievements and Enjoyments a reality, you have to plan a point in time when you will move them forward. WIN®* is the tool to do that. WIN stands for *Write It Now* in your calendar on the day you intend to do it. For example, when you decide to do something from an exercise in the upcoming section, WIN, Write It Now, in your calendar on a specific day.

The average person has many good intentions that fall through the cracks because they fail to WIN. Instead you will create more every day achievement and enjoyment if you WIN* with your desired outcomes and commitments.

To write it *now,* you need to have your calendar with you *now.* Having a calendaring device that you are comfortable using and keeping with you is a key to making sure that your decisions and commitments do not fall through the cracks.

Daily Calendars

At thirty-one years old, I was the president of a very profitable company that employed approximately 100 people. We had been experiencing growth rates that exceeded 35% a year and expected that trend to continue for several more years, which it did. We had a great team of happy people. Life was good, and I was somewhat smug.

In this setting, one of our most capable managers, Dave Ferenchick, came to me and in essence said, "Jim, you are letting a lot of us down. I know you are working hard, but many of the commitments you are making are falling through the cracks. You're not making deadlines, and some balls you are dropping altogether."

My immediate internal reaction was, "You don't know what you are talking about. We just finished another record-setting year in almost every area. I sure must be doing something right." But outwardly I tried to be calm and listen, questioning a bit what he meant.

Dave not only had brought the problem to my attention but had also come with a suggested solution. "With the way we are growing and the changes we are going through, all of us, and particularly you, Jim, have to wear lots of hats. No one can keep up with all the big and small things they commit to, unless they have an organized way to write them down." I told him I kept a pad on my desk and made lots of notes and had someone who kept my calendar. His response was that not only did I need to capture more of my commitments in my calendar myself, but I also needed to write them on the day I was going to do them. He then showed me his calendaring system and how he used it. He recommended I do the same.

When Dave left my office, I just shook my head. *Is he trying to tell me how to run my business day? Who is president of this company anyway?*

Because Dave was such a good manager, and had become a trusted friend, he had at least made me think. But I did not act right away. I continued to scratch notes on the yellow pad on my desk, on napkins in restaurants, and on scraps of paper and relied on my memory. Our business continued its growth, the demands on my time increased, and more and more things fell through the cracks.

Several months passed before Dave's continued example and my own frustration broke down my stubborn ego. I began using a calendar to immediately schedule my initial response date for my business and personal commitments. That decision and the ongoing use of a calendar have been invaluable to both my professional and my personal life.

That was more than thirty years ago. The explosion of changes and choices that has taken place in those three decades has made almost everyone's job and life situation at least as demanding as mine was decades ago.

If you are already using a *daily* calendar to consistently schedule both your business and personal desires and commitments when you make them, congratulations. I don't have to convince you of its importance. You may still find the comments in the next few paragraphs helpful. If you are not consistently using a quick-access calendar like your smart phone, tablet, or a paper calendar, then this is an encouragement to start.

If your current calendar is only on your computer, I would encourage you to also engage your phone or tablet calendar or buy a paper calendar to take with you at all times. This is what you use when your computer is not attached to you. Your always-on-hand calendar is where you catch those one out of ten things that you commit to that have been falling through the cracks. You also can and should use it to record thoughts and actions that will be critical to your Achievement and Enjoyment goals.

A growing percentage of top performers are using a smart calendar along with a small paper journal. The upscale paper notebook is now an expected swag component of TED and most top technology conferences. In addition to the ability for quick and convenient note taking, hand writing increases recall and is less distractive than phone and laptops at meetings. Just be sure to immediately follow-on with WINs in your calendar for any decisions or commitments you made.

Here's a quiz. You are at work. You decide you have a quick business question you want to ask Jerri down the hall. You leave your work area, and in the hall, you bump into Bob, who asks, "Can you get that status report to me by the end of the day Wednesday?"

You reply, "Yeah, I think so, Bob."

As you are about to get to Jerri's office, Sarah catches your attention and requests that you bring the material she loaned to you to the staff meeting in the morning. She needs to cover it with the rest of the team. You agree.

As you turn into Jerri's office, she is clearly pleased to see you because she has a number of things she would like you to follow-up on. It's fifteen minutes later before you get back to your own desk and your phone is ringing. What is the possibility that you will forget your commitment to Bob, or your promise to Sarah, or even what you went to see Jerri about?

You will not forget if you are using a daily calendar and following these three basic rules.

1. Have your calendar with you at all times. By taking your calendar with you everywhere, even when just walking down the hall to Jerri's office, you can immediately capture things you think of or agree to do.
2. WIN! (Write It Now) – Whenever you decide or agree that you need to do something, WIN on the date you intend to do it. "Return Sarah's materials" would go down for this afternoon, and "Get status report to Bob" would go on Tuesday.
3. Use your calendar every day. The commitments and priorities of your day are clearly before you to control and focus on.

When you WIN (Write It Now), it is like hitting the save button on a computer. If you have ever done extensive work on your computer only to inadvertently erase it, or lose it to a power failure, you know true frustration. The worry of repeating that mistake goes away when you hit the "Save" button. You know your work, your thought processes, are stored where you will not inadvertently lose them. WIN serves the same purpose for your mind. Knowing you have recorded what you want to do on the day and time you want to do it frees your mind from the "don't forget, don't forget" stress and worry and lets you focus on the present.

Your calendar, potentially along with a small journal, should replace the notes you write on napkins, scraps of paper, and pads on your desk or at home. Your calendar is the *one* place where you connect and can find all your activities. Use it. When you do, when you WIN with your decisions, little ones and big ones, your mind is cleared to focus on what you are currently doing. You know that your future pieces are in place, in your calendar.

It is not critical what calendar or combo you use as long as you can quickly add times and notes on the day you intend to do it. 80 percent or more of the value of a calendar comes from doing only two things:

1. WIN – Writing all important activities and commitments down on a specific day you intend to do them.
2. Opening up your calendar every day.

Some of my clients believe that 100 percent of the value of a calendar comes from just these two things. They argue that many calendar apps try to get you so enthralled with all their bells, whistles and special features, that the calendar becomes a complicated distraction. When that happens, you can retreat from using it for the key basics.

For most of us, if we WIN daily, we are getting at least 80 percent of the value of any calendaring system. If you are not routinely using a calendar now for both your business *and personal* decisions and commitments, you will be amazed at the power and control it gives you over your life.

Summary

- WIN ("Write It Now") is an essential tool to help you schedule and make progress on your Achievement and Enjoyment goals.
- To WIN effectively, be sure to have your calendar with you at all times and use it every day.
- Immediately write important activities and commitments down when you intend to do them.
- When you do, you significantly increase the likelihood of following through on your commitments.

PART TWO

Building More Meaningful Relationships

4

Gain More Achievement & Enjoyment in Every Relationship

TAP – Tool #2
Date vs. A Meeting – Tool #3

"What you leave behind is not what is engraved in stone monuments,
but what is woven into the lives of others."
— Pericles

There are essentially three functions in our lives. Master them, and you can immediately improve every relationship.

Look at the Big Picture visual below. What do you think the center circle represents?

Participants in my leadership for work and life courses have expressed dozens of different impressions, often humorous, about the center circle of the Big Picture. In many major cities, the circle is often interpreted as the outer-ring of their expressway, with the other lines in the picture being East-West and North-South routes. A manhole cover was one of the more unusual answers. More serious responses include the cycle of life or the wheel of fortune.

But the center was actually created to represent time, in the form of a clock or a watch. Time is a common element in all our past, present, and future life experiences. The happiest and most successful people have only twenty-four hours in their daily lives—no more time than anyone else. For each of us, how we choose to use our time is what will determine our levels of Achievement and Enjoyment throughout our lives.

So, what do you do with your time? What specifics make up your day—in the morning, at work, at home, and before you go to bed? If you kept a list, it would probably include many of the items below—everything from the major to the mundane.

Planning	Commuting	Watching a movie
Organizing	Meeting	Gardening
Decision making	Talking on phone	Gaming
Scheduling	Sleeping	Fishing
Problem solving	Eating	Eating
	E-mailing	Watching TV
	Showering	Playing golf
	Reading	Reading
	Chauffeuring	Hiking
	Helping with homework	Shopping
	Exercising	Playing tennis

Obviously, this is only a partial list, and everyone's list is different and varies by the day. But whether you put hundreds or thousands of items on your list, they could all be sorted into three columns.

This is because there are basically only three life functions. One is cognitive, which we commonly refer to as *Thinking*. This includes things like planning, organizing, and decision making. The second function revolves around making things happen by taking *Action*. This includes activities such as meeting, eating, and even sleeping (an action in itself!). The third function is a specific form of action that we commonly refer to as *Play*. Play includes things like watching a movie, gardening, fishing, or going on a date.

Everything we spend our time on can be sorted into these three functions:

Thinking	Acting	Playing
Planning	Commuting	Watching a movie
Organizing	Meeting	Gardening
Decision making	Talking on phone	Gaming
Scheduling	Sleeping	Fishing
Problem solving	Eating	Eating
	E-Mailing	Watching TV
	Showering	Playing golf
	Reading	Reading
	Chauffeuring	Hiking
	Helping with homework	Shopping
	Exercising	Playing tennis

Accomplishing your daily goal of Achievement and Enjoyment depends on how you balance your time among these three life functions. The easy way to remember this tool is TAP...

T = <u>Think</u>

A = <u>Act</u>

P = <u>Play</u>

Instant Chemistry

Think, Act, Play. These are the *only* things you can do to create or change a relationship. Thinking, Acting, and Playing are to a relationship what the particles of the atom are to matter. In an atom, there are electrons, protons, and neutrons. If you change the amount of one, you change the whole nature of the material—it might go from iron to copper. It becomes something entirely different simply by changing the particles.

The same is true with Think, Act, and Play. If you change the amount of one, you change the whole chemistry of any relationship. By combining these three life functions differently, you can reduce negative stress and produce a more fulfilling and balanced relationship with anyone in your life.

You can also create much richer levels of Achievement and Enjoyment across every quadrant of your life. Conversely, when you significantly neglect one or more of the TAP functions in favor of another, you become out of balance.

Take the stereotypical Over Thinker, or the "ivory tower" type. In conducting research over the years, I have been exposed to several professors who fall into this category. They think, and they think, and they think, and they do often come up with a great idea. Then what does the typical over-thinker do with it? Usually nothing—or they think about it some more or go on to think about something else. They take no action to turn it into reality.

Then there is the Over Action person, who is very busy...being busy. He or she is going all the time and usually in a hurry. They may be getting a lot of things done. But how long has it been since they stepped back and looked at where all of the going and doing is taking them? How many years has it been since they *thought* through whether their actions were really taking them where they wanted to go with their career, company, family, or their sense of self?

Then there is the stereotypical Over Player. This is the person who wakes up at sixty years old having slept on the beach by his surfboard the night before, and says, "Hey man, where did all of my buddies go?" This is the individual who has never built lasting relationships or meaningful Achievements to add pride and value to his life.

Fully understanding the value of and differences between Thinking, Acting, and Playing will enable you to positively sort all of your life's choices extremely quickly and as a result Achieve and Enjoy more fully every day. To do this, it is vital to be clear on what you identify as Think, Act, or Play.

Clarifying the Functions

Think

1. To determine by a specific *reasoning process* what new pieces you want to add to your Big Picture; 2. To determine how best to TAP into your business and personal relationships.

Most of definition number one, "to determine by a specific reasoning process," comes straight from the dictionary. TAP, as you will see, is a specific reasoning process. If you are not using some *reasoning process*, reasoning towards some conclusion, then you are by definition not thinking.

Based on this definition, should daydreaming or habitual worry be classified as Thinking?

If you answered "no," I would agree. Worry is a state of mentally buzzing back and forth and stressing over something. It rarely involves reasoning. I would encourage you to classify "worry" as Action, even though it is usually counter-productive action!

I have had senior executives tell me that prior to these clarifying definitions they believed they were great thinkers. Afterwards, they realized that they were mostly worriers. Worrying is not Thinking! To think productively you must be reasoning toward a conclusion.

What about daydreaming, that state of just letting your mind wander carefree wherever it might want to go? Which TAP function is it?

We would consider this Play. It is a fun, relaxing activity in which you are not even trying to come to a reasoned conclusion. Now, daydreaming can lead to good thinking. In that carefree state a good idea might come into your mind. At that point you might start reasoning toward a conclusion. "I might want to do that. How would I go about it?" You are then thinking. But daydreaming is not the same as Thinking.

Act

1. Gathering the pieces of your Big Picture; 2. Implementing your choices.

In taking action you are implementing your choice of what new pieces you are going to add to your Big Picture. This process of adding new pieces to your picture is never-ending. Here are some specific Action tips to make more of what you want to happen every day.

Action Tips:

1. Use a Daily Calendar. Don't just have one, use it.
2. The key to implementing your TAP choices and all your choices in life is to use the commitment tool, **WIN** from Chapter 3 with each of them.

As you will remember, WIN stands for

W - Write

I - It

N – Now…

...in your calendar *on the day* you intend to do it. This is one of the easiest tools to remember and use. And it only takes seconds.

This is the way you make a *connection in time* with the important people and things in your life. When you WIN (Write It Now), you are literally connecting the pieces of your future Big Picture. You are choosing and recording a specific day in time when you will make a desired piece of your life a reality.

3. Do It! Some helpful hints to follow Nike's old commercial advice to "Just do it!"

    a. Tell people about it. Give yourself a reputation. If you plan to start walking the stairs in your building every day at lunch, tell your co-workers, family, and friends so you feel more accountable.

    b. Start with the easy part. How many times have you put something off because you dreaded how long it was going to take? If you want to clean out the attic, just tell yourself: "I am going to just move one thing down from the attic." What happens when you move one thing? Once you start, it is much easier to keep going. End procrastination with an easy initial step. *Just* call to set the appointment, *just* bring the file up on the computer, *just* rearrange one thing in the garage.

    c. Use your calendar to WIN.

4. Whenever you commit to a project remember that more important than the finish date is the start date. WIN immediately with an initial action to begin it. Once you get started you are more than likely to keep the ball rolling and relieve the negative stress of last-minute completion pressure.

Play

1. A distinct form of Action involving no major *decision topics*; 2. A fun, relaxing, carefree activity; 3. A *celebration* of life.

Play is easy to neglect as we get older but is critical to our relationships and our sense of well-being. The TAP definition of Play includes celebration. For example, giving a co-worker a hearty handshake with a sincere, "Thanks for staying late yesterday and getting this ready for me this morning. I really needed it for my meeting," is a form of Play. We all need and want those celebratory pats on the back. If you aren't giving many of them out in each quadrant of your life, it is probably time to be more generous at work and with your family and friends. If you aren't getting enough pats on the back from others, give yourself more pats on the back more. A big part of our daily Enjoyment comes from pausing to catch ourselves and others doing things right and celebrating it.

But what about regular relaxing, goof-off, or ha-ha play. What happens if you don't play at all or play very little? The saying is "All work and no play makes Jack a dull boy." And what's true for Jack is true for Jill, too. You get dull, stressed, tense, tired, and negative. Many burn out. Studies have shown that too little play affects your health, productivity, and your ability to think and act most effectively.[3] Such a stressed state cuts time off your life and life from your time. Becoming stressed, dull, and tense also impacts the Achievement and Enjoyment, the productivity and happiness, of those around you. There is a trickle-down effect from one individual through to many others at work and at home. People become tense around you, may avoid you, and communication breaks down.

So, if you are one of those people who simply cannot justify getting some Play time just for you, if you feel too busy or guilty to do it for yourself, please do it for the rest of us! Because you become a pain in that state.

On the other side of the spectrum, what happens if you Play or celebrate too much, or goof off all the time? Quite literally, nothing happens. Achievement and productivity dissipate. It is important for you to keep the Play element of your life in balance.

---

[3] *National Institute for Play*

Date vs. Meeting – Tool #3

But what does the first definition under play mean? *No major decision topics?* It is important and immediately valuable to distinguish between each of the TAP Functions, specifically Action and Play, when interacting or scheduling time with others. In our daily lives we often perceive we are doing one, when in fact we are doing another. Before diving into a scheduled conversation or activity with someone, decide upfront whether you are going to have a Date or a Meeting.

- A *Meeting* is Action time involving *major decision topics.*
- A *Date* is Play time involving ***no** major decision topics.*

My wife has been a key executive in our business, so we have shared many important business decisions. In addition, like most married couples, we have had many other joint responsibilities, including house payments, car payments, and taking care of our children. Accordingly, we have had a lot of meetings. From time to time we agree to a "date" to just relax and enjoy each other.

Let's suppose we are out on such a romantic date complete with candlelight, a little wine, and good conversation. We might be talking about important things, like world politics.

Neither one of us is a politician, so there are no major decision topics for us. Or we may be discussing a very public trial. Since neither one of us is a lawyer, the conversation is interesting but not stressful. Or maybe I'm talking about how great she looks, or what's going to happen at the end of the evening when we get home.

So, we're laughing and romancing a little bit, and then I say, "Oh, by the way, did the guy come to fix the leak in the kitchen roof today?"

And she says, "Oh no, he didn't, and it's going to stain the entire wall. I've got to call him in the morning. Where can I write this down so I won't forget?"

What have I just done to that date?

I've changed a date into a meeting, and as a result I've changed the whole chemistry of our relationship at that moment. The unintended outcome could be a disappointing change in the chemistry at the end of the evening, too. We tend to do this all the time when we bring up major decision topics or questions regarding work, our parents' health, or a child's disappointing grade. We do it so much it becomes a habit. The result is that too many of us stop dating after we settle into a relationship. We let all our couple time together become meeting time.

The longer you stay in a relationship, the more joint responsibilities you are going to have. Because of that it is important to have meetings together.

However, if you replace all of your dates with just having meetings, then all the spark and vibrancy can go out of the relationship.

So, if you are currently involved with a significant other, or if not for future reference, remember to regularly ask yourself:

Are you still dating, or are you just having…meetings?

The difference between a Meeting and a Date applies to much more than just romantic relationships. It applies to your relationships with your friends, your co-workers, your boss, your customers, your children, and yourself.

A common business mistake I made in the past was to make all time with work associates action time. My managers would occasionally ask me to go to lunch with them. We operated in a fast-paced, positive, make-it-happen environment. I knew they usually used lunch as a time for rest and relaxation. They wanted to get recharged before returning to the intensity of our office. But I always went to lunch with a business agenda. They would be talking about the ballgame, or the camping trip they went on, and when there was an opening, I would say something like, "By the way, Pat, how did third shift do last night?" or "Dave, what did West Coast sales look like last week?"

When I asked those "decision topic" questions, it changed the whole tone of the lunch. It was apparent my co-workers didn't have a very good "Date." I didn't have a very well-received meeting. And do you know what else happened? They quit asking me to lunch.

It took me a while to get the message, but I finally learned. We began to agree up front as to the purpose of lunch. Was it to be a business "meeting," or were we going to put business aside for a short time? What we commonly did was to agree to get the business topics out of the way before the food came and then just relax while we ate. This gave everyone permission to lay back during the meal rather than be ready at every second for the business ball that might be thrown their way.

"Meetings" and "dates" can and should be valuable experiences. When you spend time with your children, your parents, your siblings, or friends, deciding ahead of time whether you want an Action or Play focus, whether you want to have a "Meeting" or a "Date," will greatly impact the value of those moments.

Play Means...

- No major decision topics for anyone involved. Have a *Date*, not a *Meeting*.
- Avoiding interruptions that disrupt being in a Play state.
- Celebrating each other, the activity of the moment, your surroundings, and the Achievements that led you to this state of Play. Celebrating life!

The distinctions between Thinking, Acting, and Playing are essential. It may seem simple, but if we don't consider or understand them, we may believe we are doing one, when in fact we are doing another.

To clarify the differences, below is a helpful exercise. Identify each specific activity below as *primarily* Think, Act, or Play. Then check your answers in the key below. There is almost always some overlap among Think, Act, or Play so consider the *primary* function involved. For example, crossing the street is primarily action, although obviously there is some degree of thinking. Focus on what function is primarily involved in completing each.

Think, Act, or Play?

T, A, or P

1. Having a meeting with your boss _____

2. Having your boss over for a barbecue _____

3. Taking a Sunday drive _____

4. Driving to work _____

5. Having a candlelight dinner with your date or spouse _____

6. Planning your input at the staff meeting _____

7. Dreaming of buying a new home _____

8. Planning customer presentation to sell on your solution _____

9. Reading the Wall Street Journal _____

10. Reading a suspense novel _____

11. Dreaming of success in your business _____

12. Congratulating/thanking a co-worker _____

13. Helping your child with homework _____

14. Watching TV with your kids _____

1.A 2.P 3.P 4.A 5.P 6.T 7.P 8.T 9.A 10.P 11.P 12.P 13.A 14.P

Often, number one ("Having a meeting with your boss") is identified as Thinking. When should the thinking for a meeting with your boss be done? Before the meeting. Although all meetings involve some thinking, most meetings are *primarily* for Action. Meetings are designed to deliver information to others and to listen to information given to you, to inform a decision or make progress towards a goal. Unfortunately, too many meetings end up being thinking-by-talking-out-loud-meetings because the parties involved do not adequately think *ahead of time*. Meetings that should primarily be Think time are the very few that are specifically designated as brainstorming.

Number four ("Driving to work") is often debated and labeled as Thinking. Your commute may be so routine that you do some thinking on the way to work. But the actual steering of the car, the driving itself, is Action. However, number three, "taking a Sunday drive," implies a different purpose, which is Play.

Number nine, "Reading the Wall Street Journal," for most people represents the Action of reading and gathering information. In the process of reading, your mind may be triggered by an article or stock price. Then you may begin Thinking, *That's a company I own some shares in. I ought to think about buying some more.* But the reading itself is Action. If you read the newspaper for pleasure and to appreciate the quality of the writing it contains, then Play would have been an appropriate answer to this question.

The word in numbers seven and eleven that makes them Play is "dreaming." Number thirteen, "Helping with homework," is mostly Action.

The Balance Watch

There is Always a Face on Your Watch

Just like there are twelve numbers on a watch that tell you how much time you have in a day, there are twelve letters in Think, Act, and Play that tell you what you are primarily doing with that time. And like all watches, your Balance Watch has a "face" on it.

Whatever you are doing, you are doing it with or for some individual or a group of individuals. It could be for your customer, your boss, the next department, your spouse, your child, or yourself. Even when you are working alone on a particular project, there is a face on your watch. There is someone you are doing that project for, or an end-user. For example, as I am writing this, you and other potential readers are the "Face" on my watch. Whatever you are doing, you should always keep in focus the "Face" on your watch.

You have a limited amount of time in your life. How you spend it, and who you spend it with, will shape your Achievements and Enjoyments. Thinking, Acting, and Playing each have an important role in determining those outcomes. How you choose to balance them with the people in your life, and throughout your life, is up to you.

The TAP tool makes that easy. Now it's time to apply it for immediate results. As you continue reading, I encourage you to take advantage of the examples and the **sixty-second to two-minute** TAP exercises that follow in the next chapter. They are powerfully quick and simple.

Read through the examples and then have fun with the applications for each of your life quadrants. The more TAPs you complete and act on as you go through the chapters, the more automatically you will use the tools every day for the rest of your life. By finishing them you will be writing your own story, scripting your future Big Picture with more Achievement and Enjoyment. You will also multiply the retention and ongoing value you receive from reading this book.

Enjoy!

Summary

- How you choose to use your time is what determines how much you Achieve and Enjoy during it.
- Your time is spent on three functions: Thinking, Acting, or Playing (TAP).
- These three functions, or TAP, are the *only* things you can do to create or change your relationships.
- There is always a "Face" on your watch. Be sure and keep it in focus.
- Effectively balancing TAP can immediately improve your relationships and produces much higher levels of Achievement and Enjoyment.

5

TAP® Into Your Family & Friends

"When you love someone, the best thing you can offer is your presence.
How can you love if you are not there?
— Thich Nhat Hanh

TAP is a quick and easy thinking tool you will use to achieve more and enjoy more with all the people in your life, including yourself. With repeated use it becomes an instinctive way to create more value, happiness, and balance in every relationship.

Initially, I encourage you to do the exercises in writing to get a clear understanding of how the TAP Process works. Once you have done it on paper a few times, you will graduate to using it as a mental tool to use throughout your normal day. To get started, please read through the TAP steps on the next page and then the example applications that follow.

Daily TAP Process

1. Put *one* Face on your Balance Watch.

The Balance Watch

2. Determine whether you've been *Thinking, Acting*, or *Playing* enough in this relationship.
3. Decide if that's OK.
4. Determine which TAP Function to emphasize in this relationship now.
5. Choose the specific option to improve your Thinking, Acting, or Playing and WIN with it in your daily calendar.

Shown on the next page is an example of TAP in the Family Quadrant. Illustrated are my mental steps in TAPing into my daughter Amanda, who was fifteen at the time of this example. This occurred on a Sunday. I had stopped by my office and was about to leave for home.

TAP Exercise – Family

1. I put **Amanda's** face on my mental watch and asked myself:

2. **"Have I been Thinking about Amanda enough lately?"**
    (Yes)/No

    Yes, I've been thinking about her a lot. I've been thinking that she is fifteen going on twenty-five and putting as much distance between herself and her father as she can.

    "Have I been Acting with Amanda enough lately?"   (Yes)/No
    Yes. I've been helping her with some homework projects, so that's OK.

    "Have I had any Play time with Amanda lately"   Yes/(No)
    No, not recently.

3. **"Is that OK?"**   Yes/(No)
    No, it's not. Vikki and I want her to grow up to be independent and self-sufficient, but the gap she has managed to create is a little too wide. It's not OK.

4. **"Which TAP Functions do I need to emphasize now?"**
    Think/Act/(Play)

We need a little Play time together now.

5. **"What specific Play thing should I do?" Decide, then WIN with it.**
    I'll ask Amanda to spend some goof-off time with me tonight.

In less than sixty seconds I had decided I wanted and needed play time with Amanda and picked up the phone to call her to set something up. Now, my daughters have understood since they were four years old the difference between a date and a meeting. When I would say, "Hey, girls, would you like to go to McDonald's with Daddy?" they would put their hands on their hips and in a very serious tone say, "Daddy, is this a date...or is this a meeting?" They wanted to know upfront whether we were going for fun or if it was going to be one of those life-lesson things.

So, I called Amanda and told her I would like to have a brief *date* with her, just some play time. We could either go out for a quick bite to eat or just hang out at the house together.

Her predictable response was, "Not tonight. I've got so much homework to do and my favorite TV show is on." With persistence we agreed we could "not go out for a date" but that we would get a few relaxed minutes together..."If I have time, Dad."

My response to this enthusiastic reception was to take out my calendar for Sunday evening, and write in caps **PLAY TIME WITH AMANDA**.

When I arrived home, Amanda was watching TV. "Not now, Dad, this is my favorite show." My guess is that whatever was on at the time would have qualified as her favorite show. I wanted to make some phone calls and had some work to do around the house, so I said fine. But I made it a point to leave my calendar open on the kitchen counter with that big reminder jumping out at me.

I came back to Amanda several times that evening, but she was always involved doing something important—homework, talking on the phone, watching another favorite show. Finally, I was ready to go to bed and I said, "Amanda, I'm getting ready to go to bed. Can you just come sit with me for a little while in the living room?"

"Oh, all right."

We just sat and chatted for maybe ten minutes. I don't remember exactly what we chatted about, but I'm sure of what we did not discuss. I did not ask about her grades, or chores, or boyfriends. *No major decision topics.* She did show me where she had her tooth pulled earlier in the week, which I hadn't seen. After a relaxed conversation, we said good night.

The next morning as I got ready to leave for the airport and Amanda prepared to go to school, she asked me, "Dad, can you take me shopping tonight?" Now, if you have ever had a teenage daughter, you can probably relate to the startling nature of this question. My teenage daughter was asking me, her father, to take her shopping! Now she was probably thinking, "If Mom has a credit card, Dad has a credit card." I told her I couldn't do it that night, as I was flying out of town, and instead we set a shopping date for the next week.

Now what had happened the night before? TAP had narrowed the gap between father and daughter just enough to where she would actually spend some of my money. That was progress.

The next week we went out to a funky little area of Atlanta called Little Five Points. As it turned out she didn't spend any of my money except for dinner. Instead we ended up doing that window-shopping thing, which I've never fully understood. We had a delightful evening and now that she's older, she occasionally calls her Dad and asks him for a date.

Now why do I give you this small example? I can give you breathtaking examples of individuals who got a promotion, landed a huge account, and steered a friend out of addiction by using TAP. I don't give those examples because most of life is not made up of those big pieces that fall into place. Most of your life and mine are made up of those little pieces, those small connections we make every day. TAP is a way to make sure you consciously put in place those positive pieces on a daily basis, big and small. And you never know; sometimes what you think is a minor piece turns out to be a big one to someone else and your relationship.

That was a family quadrant TAP example. Let's take a quick look at a Friend's TAP. During a training session at his company, John put his friend Rob's face on his Balance Watch. He answered the TAP questions as follows:

Have I been Thinking about Rob?

"Yes, I think about Rob fairly often. He was my best friend in college, and we roomed together for three of our four years in school."

Have I been Acting with Rob?

"No. Rob moved from Atlanta to Chicago about two years ago, and I've had no connection with him in the last eighteen months."

Have I had any Play time with Rob?

"No, I haven't even messaged him in a year-and-a-half."

Is that OK?

This is an important question. He could have readily decided "Yes, that's OK. Rob's going in his direction; I'm going in mine," but his quick, thoughtful answer was, "No! That's not OK. Rob was not only my best college friend, he is one of, if not the best friend I ever had."

Predetermine which TAP Function to emphasize now.

He circled Act and Play.

Choose the specific alternative and WIN with it in your calendar.

"I just need to call Rob." He knew from Rob's Facebook page that he was still single. He figured if it was the old Rob, he would be sleeping in on a Saturday morning, so he put a WIN in his calendar for Saturday at 10:00 a.m. to "Call Rob."

We had a follow up session with his company about two months later, and he told us how his TAP worked. He said, "I called Rob, and as soon as he picked up the phone, we started bantering just like we were still in college." Rob said he thought of him often because he had a client in Atlanta, and every time he flew in he said to himself, "I should have called you." Well, the next time he had an Atlanta trip, the two of them got together. They started and still routinely phone each other at least once a week. Our client had also made reservations to travel to Chicago and spend a long weekend with Rob.

Instead of showing up at the fiftieth college reunion and saying, "Rob…is that you?", a simple TAP kept their friendship from getting caught in an "As Soon As" Trap. They now regularly put a piece of enjoyment and support into each other's life picture with a call, text, or visit.

Good Ideas Are Not Enough

We all have good ideas all the time. But just thinking something through to a good decision is not enough unless you make the connection in time when it will happen. Make sure you create that *connection* with the important individuals in your life—business and personal—by writing a specific activity in your calendar at a specific time. WIN: Write It Now.

Please don't be like so many clients who use their daily calendars only for business. You calendar business appointments and to do's because they are too important to forget. Is that not equally true of your desired personal achievements and enjoyments? If you don't commit your time to what's most important in all four quadrants, then less important things will fill it up.

Don't shortchange your spouse, your friends, your family, your work, or yourself. TAP into them and WIN to insure you avoid the as-soon-as-trap.

Your Turn

Take one minute now to TAP into someone important in *either* your Family or Friends quadrant. Write his or her name on the top of the exercise or on a piece of paper. Go through the TAP questions. Pick which TAP function to emphasize. Choose the specific thing you want to do and write it in your calendar on the day you expect to take the first step on it.

It might be a Play "date" you want to have with your spouse or significant other. (Remember, no decision topics). Maybe it's some action that's been requested by a family member or friend—clean out the garage; review college options; help install the new app. And don't forget parents and grandparents. TAPing into them in a different way can often be very meaningful to them and you.

Once you sort between Think, Act or Play, usually the specific thing you want to do will jump right out at you. In those rarer TAPs when you know you want to do something but you need to plan out more specifically your Action or Play, then you need to WIN with "Think time" to plan those next steps.

You will probably find a minute is enough time to complete your first TAP. Once you finish that initial TAP, do one or two more with other important individuals in the Family or Friends/Community quadrant. I encourage you to do these initial TAP exercises in writing, as doing so creates a much stronger synaptic connection that aids memory recall. Do four of these TAP exercises in writing and you will probably never forget this balance tool.

You will know you are through with your first TAP application when you WIN with it. If you do not have a calendar with you now that you use, send yourself an email or text to get a calendar and enter your WIN priorities.

Have fun with this. TAP into a few of the important people in your Family or Friends/Community quadrants now using the TAP worksheets on the following pages or download and print free TAP worksheets for your individual use at worklifebalance.com/worksheets.

TAP Exercise - Family

1. Put one Face on your Watch and check your relationship with

_____ .

2. Determine whether you've been Thinking, Acting or Playing enough in this relationship.

Thinking	Yes/No
Acting	Yes/No
Playing	Yes/No

3. Decide if that's OK.   Yes/No

4. Pre-determine which Tap Function to emphasize in this relationship now.

Think/Act/Play

5. Choose a specific alternative to improve your Thinking, Action or Play, and WIN (Write it Now) in your calendar.

TAP Exercise - Friends and Community

1. Put one Face on your Watch and check your relationship with

_____ .

2. Determine whether you've been Thinking, Acting or Playing enough in this relationship.

Thinking	Yes/No
Acting	Yes/No
Playing	Yes/No

3. Decide if that's OK. Yes/No

4. Pre-determine which Tap Function to emphasize in this relationship now.

Think/Act/Play

5. Choose a specific alternative to improve your Thinking, Action or Play, and WIN (Write it Now) in your calendar.

If you decided to TAP into someone only in one quadrant, Family or Friends/Community, why not TAP into someone in the other quadrant now?

If you took a minute or two to TAP, you should have one or two items in your calendar. Do you think you will follow through and actually do what you wrote down? Do you think it will be helpful to your relationship with that person if you do? Would you have done what you wrote down, if you hadn't used the TAP tool to begin with?

Doing Important Things That Would Not Have Gotten Done

From asking these same questions of thousands of individuals immediately after they complete this exercise, we've gathered some consistent and valuable feedback. Almost everyone who has put their TAP decisions into their calendar thinks they will follow through and expect that doing so will prove valuable to their relationships. Follow-up studies show that more than 90 percent of those who did TAP and then WIN followed through and found this benefit.

Most individuals do not think they would have taken the step they selected without having used TAP. This is true even though a significant percentage followed through on something they had considered doing previously. Sometimes TAP produces a new idea. Most of the time, however, you arrive at something that has previously gone through your mind. Yet using the TAP tool enables you to sort through the options floating in your brain very quickly, decide whether or not you want to act on them, and WIN with your conclusion.

Doing Important Things Sooner

Another common response we receive is, "I probably would have done this anyway, but not as soon. I'm not sure when I would have gotten around to it." This is an important aspect of TAP: getting valuable things done sooner. At a recent seminar, a father had decided to TAP into his young daughter and WIN, resulting in him assembling her bike the next day. When I asked him if that wasn't something he would have done anyway, he responded, "Well, she's been after me for three weeks to do it, and I haven't gotten it done. Yes, I would have eventually gotten around to it, but not as soon. When I do it tomorrow, without her asking me again, it is going to mean so much more to her than if she had nagged me about it weeks from now." And it did.

Good intentions delivered too late have a very diminished effect. Sometimes they even have a negative effect on building the relationship. Conversely, doing it sooner rather than later multiplies the value of the personal and professional connections that thoughtful ideas produce. By using TAP to quickly sort, you will be able to select and act on those good intentions much sooner and produce much more positive results.

Kent Williams is the president of a national automotive parts distributor, an active tennis player, a husband, and a dad. Like all of us, he stays busy. At the time Kent brought these tools into his company, it was going through significant, positive changes. Kent's business plate was very full and very time-consuming. A few weeks after Kent started using TAP, he was putting it to use in the family quadrant.

He put the face of his eleven-year-old son, Scott, on the watch. With all his work activities Kent concluded he hadn't gotten enough Play time with Scott lately. He was able to WIN on an upcoming Friday afternoon to take Scott to a National League baseball game. Kent blocked out the whole afternoon and evening as Play time with Scott. After a fun time at the game, Scott asked, "What are we going to do now, Dad?"

"What would you like to do Scott?"

"Could I pitch to you in the backyard?"

"Sure."

Afterwards Kent and Scott went to dinner, just the two of them. Towards the end of dinner, Scott said, "Dad, can I borrow your pen?" He started to draw on a napkin. Scott had seen the Happiness Meter®

his Dad had brought home from his seminar. This is a fun gauge with an arrow that can be moved between five faces that graduate from a giant frown to a giant smile. (See Chapter 15). On the napkin Scott was creating a revised version.

The meter he drew showed the arrow not just up to the biggest smile, but way past it. There were springs popping out of the meter at the top and bottom like a watch that had been wound too tightly and blew out of its casings. As he handed his drawing to Kent, Scott said, "Dad, you made me so happy. I have had so much fun today—you broke my Happiness Meter."

Kent gave me a copy of that napkin, which I still have. It reminds me of the value of those important connections. I need to make them, you need to make them, we all need to make them often with those important people in our lives.

Remember, life is like a puzzle with an infinite number of pieces. Each tool we will cover serves as a sorting mechanism. The Big Picture helps you sort to one of the quadrants that you want to focus on improving. The TAP process gets you focused on an individual in that quadrant. The three TAP functions, Think, Act, Play, help you identify the specific thing to do to better connect with that person. Don't stop there or you've wasted your time. The WIN tool helps you prioritize and commit to doing it on a specific date. With these tools, you can do all of this great work in less time than it took you to read this paragraph.

Summary

- TAP is a tool to help create more value and balance in every relationship.
- Consider the relationships you want to enhance in your personal life, devise a TAP plan, and be sure to WIN with your next steps.
- It's easy to lose sight of important relationships when life gets busy, but good intentions delivered too late have a very diminished effect.
- TAP allows you to focus on your intentions and produce more positive results quicker, helping you avoid the "As Soon As" Trap in important relationships.

6

TAP
Into Your Work Associates

"People who work together will win, whether it be against complex football defenses, or the problems of a modern society."
— Vincent Thomas Lombardi

Each of us has both internal and external customers at work. Your external customer is the purchaser of the goods or services your organization produces. Your internal customers are those individuals, departments, or organizations that depend on you to provide them with support to get their job done well. These internal customer connections are linked both ways. For example, a manager is a customer for productive, quality work and ideas from the people who report to her. Going in the other direction, those who report to her are customers for her leadership, direction, development, and motivation.

Who are your internal customers where you work?

Initially you may think of those individuals in your department, or the next department your work flows to—your immediate peers. These are the people you impact most on a day-to-day basis. Now zoom out to your whole work quadrant. In that broader sense you are connected to everyone in your organization in delivering results for external and internal customers. We all serve as ambassadors for our organization externally and internally, helping to create a work environment that our colleagues can enjoy achieving in. Work environments where

Achievement *and* Enjoyment are high consistently provide a more positive, high-quality experience for everyone involved.

To manage this well, it requires you to regularly TAP into your internal and external customers. In doing so it is important to recognize the direct relationship between the act of *communicating* and customer satisfaction.

Active *Listening* is the Most Critical Part of Communication.

Wise employees and wise managers listen to both their external and their internal customers. This is true not only in your business but in every part of your life. As simple and as obvious as this sounds, it is extremely important. It is so important that corporations spend millions of dollars every year to send employees and managers to training courses to learn how to listen better. You can reap similar benefits by following the simple steps below.

To TAP into our work associates effectively, we must first recognize and respect both our external and internal clients by listening.

<u>After</u> you have listened, make sure you understand the person and are ready to act on what you learn by:

- Asking clarifying questions.
- After they are answered say "I understand," then **repeat** the key points as you understand them clearly, concisely and positively.
- WIN with the appropriate information or follow-up items.

Here's an example of the process. Jake stops John in the hall and states, "John, I need that report you are working on for a meeting Friday morning and I need a column formatting of a,b,c,y,x."

John asks a few clarification questions and then repeats what he thinks he has heard. "OK, Jake. I understand. You need this report by Friday morning and you want it formatted a,b,c,x,y."

"NO, NO! My meeting is at 8:00 a.m. Friday morning away from the office. I need the report Thursday afternoon so I can review it. And the format needs to be a,b,c,*y,x*," Jake states emphatically.

At this point what does John need to do to make sure full and correct communications have occurred?

He needs to repeat Jake's message again. "I understand now. You need this by Thursday afternoon at the latest and you want it formatted a,b,c,y,x. I'll get it done."

To make sure this assignment doesn't fall through the cracks or become a last-minute fire, John WINs with a 30-minute block in his calendar Wednesday morning to reformat the report and get it to Jake.

Good listening is the key to good communications. Consistent follow-through is the key to making good communications pay off.

If you talk too much, you can't listen well. Mark Twain told a story that began with a man chiding his friend, "I think it is a shame that you have not spoken to your wife for fifteen years. How do you explain it? How do you justify it?"

That poor man said, "I didn't want to interrupt her."

Let's not be so anxious to talk. Hopefully, we can help teach all those we influence, especially ourselves, that listening should go both ways.

Listening Occurs Almost Automatically When You TAP

Two-way listening will occur almost automatically when you TAP. What follows is a TAP application done by one of our clients that illustrates the point. As president of his small firm he was in his office and decided to apply the TAP tool to Sue, his office manager and the team member he depended on the most.

"Have I been Thinking about Sue lately? Yes, I think about what a great job she does all the time. She is clearly the most valuable person I have working here."

"Have I been Acting with Sue lately? No, but I don't have to. Sue really runs this place day to day. She keeps the ball rolling for all of us."

"Have I had any Play time with Sue lately? Taken her to lunch or given her a pat on the back? No, not really, but one great thing about Sue is that she is self-motivated, so upbeat. She doesn't seem to need that kind of thing."

To the question, "Is that OK?" his initial mental reply was, "Sure that's OK. Sue's doing a great job." He began to TAP into somebody else.

Then he stopped, and mentally stepped back to Sue. "You know, other than Thinking about Sue, which she doesn't know I've done, I have not really TAPed into her at all. I think I'll just go say "Hi" to Sue and ask her how things are going. He did not have to WIN because he immediately acted on it. He got up, went to Sue's desk, which was right outside his office, and pulled up a chair. As he sat down, he asked Sue, "How are things going?"

Sue looked at him a little strangely, since it was unusual for her boss to stop by her office unannounced. She hesitated a bit and then said, "Well…not that good." She then opened the center drawer in her desk, pulled out a piece of paper, and handed it to him. It was her resignation.

When he was retelling the story to me, he was still panicked. He had been shocked by her resignation. "I don't understand this, Sue. Why in the world would you be thinking of leaving? You are the most valuable person I have working here. You are like the hub of the wheel; this place revolves around you. Everybody here loves you and the work you do."

Sue just looked at him blankly for a few seconds—time that I'm sure seemed like an eternity to this entrepreneur. Then she quietly said, "Nobody ever told me that. I never knew."

He immediately asked her to join him in his office. After again declaring very clearly and emphatically her value to him and the firm, he listened. He really listened. Interestingly enough she had no major complaints. Instead she had a number of very good suggestions she had never been able to get his ear for, most of which were implemented in the coming months. And Sue stayed.

If Sue had left, it would have cost this small firm tens, maybe hundreds of thousands of dollars. It might have even cost the owner the firm itself. Instead, they have not only survived but grown substantially. And since this owner is a strong leader, he now makes it a habit to TAP into all his key people on a regular basis. The Action he most often focuses on is listening.

Play Includes Catching People Doing Something Right

The executive above not only Acted by listening; he also Played by complimenting and celebrating how valuable Sue was to him and the organization. We all want and need this throughout our lives.

Several years ago, my wife Vikki and I were attending a student assembly at our daughters' elementary school. Towards the end of the assembly, the principal of the school strode to the front of the room with a serious look on his face. With great concern, he looked out over the 300 students who ranged in age from six to twelve, and said, "You've done it again, and we caught you. And it involves quite a number of you, and it is important that we address it."

I was concerned, wanting to hear about this problem that involved such a large number of students. I was somewhat perplexed, though, because the students, especially the younger ones, were giggling. The principal went on in a serious tone.

"Mrs. Jack caught Johnny Miller holding the door for his classmates as they went into the lunch room."

"Leslie Harrell, Amanda Hart, Emily Crosby, Katherine Swartz, and Shirley Washington were all caught by Mrs. Samples, talking quietly at the lunchroom table."

"Mrs. Spencer caught Leslie Johnson saying please and thank you when she came up to the office to get some supplies for her classroom."

"Mrs. Wright and I have caught the entire fourth grade class doing a wonderful, caring job working with their kindergarten buddies."

"And we're not going to stop. We are going to keep our eyes and ears open every day to catch you, too."

It was clear those kids knew what was coming as soon as their principal started speaking, and they loved it. We all appreciate and need positive feedback. Whether we are four or forty, eighteen or eighty-one, we all want to regularly be caught doing something right. Use TAP to remind yourself to include this celebration and congratulation side of Play to strengthen that relationship and encourage positive performance and character. Remember when you praise improvement it motivates that person to keep on improving.

TAP Into an External Client

TAP is equally effective with external customers and can greatly enhance the value organizations derive from client relationships. Here is how it works:

TAP Exercise – Work

1. Richard, the head of sales at a mid-sized organization, put a key prospective customer, Phil, on his mental watch and asked:

2. "Have I been Thinking about Phil enough lately?" (Yes)/No
Yes, we have been doing a great deal of thinking together on how to bring our product to his firm.

"Have I been Acting with Phil enough lately?" (Yes)/No
Yes and no. "Yes" because we have met several times. But "No" because the last meeting had no Next Step. Things are hanging.

"Have I had any Play time with Phil lately" (Yes)/No
Yes. My wife and I had recently enjoyed dinner with him and his wife.

3. "Is that OK?" Yes/(No)
No. The strong interest of the client will wane if I don't stay behind it.

4. "Which TAP Functions do I need to emphasize now?"
Think/(Act)/Play

I need to Act.

5. "What specific Action do I need to do?" Decide, then WIN with it.
Send an email with next steps. In it I will offer to provide a preview of our product to Phil's other senior officers to gain additional executive buy-in on moving ahead.

The head of sales opened his calendar to WIN, scheduling time a few days later to think about write and send the email. Within one week, Phil called him to arrange a meeting to preview the product for his organization. Within one month, that organization purchased the product and became one of the company's largest accounts. If Richard had not taken a few minutes to TAP and WIN on a timely basis, that potential could have been lost.

Take three minutes now to TAP into an internal or external customer by completing one of the written exercises below. Internally consider your boss or someone you know who deserves a pat on the back or a rest-and-relaxation lunch. It could be a supplier or an entire department or team that deserves some thanks. Externally, it could be a specific customer you could TAP into more positively or something you could do to positively impact your customers in general. Be sure to WIN with your specific activity in your calendar.

Use the TAP worksheets on the following pages or download and print free TAP worksheets for your individual use at worklifebalance. com/worksheets.

TAP Exercise - Work

1. Put one Face on your Watch and check your relationship with

_____ .

2. Determine whether you've been Thinking, Acting or Playing enough in this relationship.

Thinking	Yes/No
Acting	Yes/No
Playing	Yes/No

3. Decide if that's OK.   Yes/No

4. Pre-determine which Tap Function to emphasize in this relationship now.

Think/Act/Play

5. Choose a specific alternative to improve your Thinking, Action or Play, and WIN (Write it Now) in your calendar.

If you WIN with these exercises as you read the book, it will cement the process in your mind in a way that creates a life-long daily habit.

I'd like to share one last story from Teresa, an engineer for a rapidly growing design firm. She saw a 90% increase in her work output within a month of using TAP. Even more significantly, her engineering team's productivity increased by 300%! How could these simple tools produce such dramatic increases in productivity in what was already a high-performing department?

Teresa was a recent hire out of college. She felt that the senior engineer responsible for delegating work in her department had avoided giving her challenging work because he did not know her well. She decided to TAP into him and realized there had been Thinking and Action (mostly on low level projects), but neither knew anything about the other individual personally. To change this, Teresa put some Play into their relationship. The next opportunity she had, Teresa commented on what she thought was a valuable personal side of the senior engineer's life. "I've heard you talking on the phone with what seems like young children. It looks like you enjoy them a lot. Are they your children?"

This senior engineer beamed and began enthusiastically talking. No, he didn't have children. It was his niece and nephew he had been talking to. He was their soccer coach and had a great relationship with them. Teresa asked questions, listened for a few minutes, and enjoyed learning more about what made her co-engineer tick.

As a result of opening up their personal communication, they also had more productive business communication. The delegating engineer's confidence in Teresa increased. Instead of just giving her C-level work, she began getting important A-level assignments. Because of that, many bottlenecks throughout the department were broken. Teresa wrote to us: "If something doesn't appear to be going right with someone, I TAP into them to determine what needs to be done, WIN with it, then follow through." Others in her department are now doing the same, and the team has multiplied their Achievement *and* their Enjoyment substantially.

Make TAP a habit in your business life, in addition to your personal life, and you will see similar benefits.

Summary

- Each of us has both "internal" and "external" customers where we work.
- Regularly TAP into these customers using the TAP tool to balance your Thinking, Acting, and Playing in every relationship.
- Don't forget to Play, which includes catching people doing something right and then recognizing and showing gratitude for their positive actions.
- Active Listening skills are critical to making TAP effective—listen, repeat what was heard, and WIN with specific actions for any follow up.

7

TAP Into Yourself

"The function of man is to live his life. The function of a man with high standards is to live his live well."
— Aristotle

Up to this point, you have had the opportunity to TAP into someone at work, in your family, and among your friends. Who's left in your Big Picture?

If you answered "myself," congratulations for recognizing that *you* deserve to be part of your own Big Picture. Too often we leave ourselves out. We fill our lives with only duties and obligations. This can lead to an increasingly gray existence.

For many of us, when we start to do something just for ourselves, guilt raises its ugly head and says, "How dare you indulge yourself in this purely personal waste of time when you have all these pressing commitments and responsibilities?"

Well, guess what? It is not only OK, it is virtuous to take some time just for you. If you are going to be there for all the important people in your life, you have to stay mentally, physically, and spiritually healthy.

It is not only virtuous, it is absolutely essential that you TAP into yourself on a regular basis for a successful Big Picture. Here's how to get started:

- **Think:** Determine your immediate and long term "Self" priorities by using a reasoning process.

- **Take Action**: Exercise; Set a doctor's appointment; Get more sleep; Eat right; Sign up for the course... Whatever it is, start with your first action now.
- **Play:** Read; Daydream; Pursue your hobbies and pleasures; Shop... Play is important to a healthy self, too!

To Achieve and Enjoy in your Work, Family, Friends and Community, you must regularly take some quality TAP time for yourself to Think, Act, and Play. The next page contains a Self TAP example that was completed by the president of a non-profit association.

TAP Exercise – Self

1. Dustin put his own face on the watch and asked:

2. Have I been Thinking about myself lately? (Yes)/ No
Yes. I've been thinking that I've gained about 25 lbs. over the last two years and I'm not very happy about it.

Have I been Acting enough when it comes to me? Yes /(No)
No, I haven't done anything about it.

Have I been Playing enough? (Yes)/ No
Well, I sure love to eat and I've obviously been doing plenty of that.

3. Is that OK? Yes /(No)
No, not really. I am really uncomfortable and would like to get this weight off.

4. Of the three TAP Functions, what do I need to emphasize?
Think /(Act)/ Play
I need to emphasize Action to lose this weight.

5. *The specific actions I need to take are to get back on that food program I lost weight with several years ago and to exercise regularly.*

Dustin took out his calendar and scheduled to call and order the food plan he had used in the past. In addition, he planned to walk regularly. Dustin had decided that the best time for him to walk was in the evenings after work. He could not determine in advance what evenings they would be, due to the nature of his work obligations. He had decided, however, to walk at least three times a week.

He did not just write down "Walk" on one day. Obviously, one day of exercise would not shed 25 lbs. Nor did he write reminders on every day—an easy thing to do on your cell phone. If he did, he knew that the word would become like the lines on the page, something he would get so used to seeing that he would overlook them. Instead, he wrote "WALK" in his calendar every *other* day as a reminder for a month. He wrote it in at 6 o'clock, the time he expected to do it.

About three months after Dustin wrote those reminders in his calendar, he called me to say he had lost his 25 lbs. That was almost three years ago. He has kept the weight off. At times he has added 7 or 8 lbs. back on. But by TAPING into himself on a regular basis, he has been able to get back on the right eating and exercise track and maintain his health and weight.

Writing these periodic reminders in your calendar, as Dustin did, is a success pattern that dates back for centuries. Benjamin Franklin credited a similar approach as the *one thing* he owed all his success and happiness to. At the beginning of each year Franklin would identify thirteen characteristics about himself that he wanted to focus on to improve to the point of mastery. He would then focus his attention on one characteristic each week for thirteen weeks. He would then repeat the entire process four times a year. If Franklin were alive today, he would tell you that by concentrating on one thing at a time, you will get farther with it in one week than you otherwise would in a year.

Now, it is your turn to TAP into yourself. Put your face on the watch below and step through the questions until you arrive at a WIN. If it's something you want to be an ongoing effort, schedule it several times in your calendar.

Use the TAP worksheets on the following pages or download and print free TAP worksheets for your individual use at worklifebalance. com/worksheets.

TAP Exercise - Self

1. Put one Face on your Watch and check your relationship with

_____ .

2. Determine whether you've been Thinking, Acting or Playing enough both in and about your life.

Thinking	Yes/No
Acting	Yes/No
Playing	Yes/No

3. Decide if that's OK.   Yes/No

4. Pre-determine which Tap Function to emphasize now.

Think/Act/Play

5. Choose a specific alternative to improve your Thinking, Action or Play, and WIN (Write it Now) in your calendar.

Did you decide to treat yourself with a shopping trip, outdoor activity, or some play experience you have been putting off? Was it an action to improve your physical, mental, educational, or spiritual well-being? Or did you identify something around the house or yard that you want to get done for yourself? Whatever you decided, it probably jumped out at you in less than a minute. It does not take long to make those positive connections. When your WIN date comes up, enjoy making it happen.

Summary

- Determine whether you have been Thinking, Acting, or Playing enough.
- Then decide on an action plan and WIN with it in your calendar.
- For ongoing goals, set periodic reminders in your calendar to help you follow through consistently.
- It is essential to TAP into yourself regularly to achieve your desired Big Picture—and to be happy and healthy for the important people in it!

8

Capturing the Magic of the Moment
A.M. & P.M. – Tool #4

"To listen closely and reply well is the highest perfection we are able to attain in the art of conversation."
— Francois de La Rocheoucauld

The final tool in this section helps you capture the magic and value of each moment with clarity and ease. Just like TAP begins with putting a face on your watch, this tool is centered around time and how to best utilize it throughout your days and your lifetime. The tool is called "A.M. & P.M." These are words you use every day, but, when used to help focus, the terms take on an important new meaning:

A.M. = Activity of the Moment
P.M. = Person of the Moment

This is an exceptionally valuable tool. It will greatly increase your Achievement and Enjoyment in every aspect of your life.

After explaining A.M. & P.M. to the president of a large regional bank, he said, "Jim, if I could just get that across to all of the people in our organization: when you are with someone, really be with them. It is one of the most valuable personal and professional characteristics there is."

Too often we shortchange the present by worrying about the past or the future. We are so concerned about the meeting we just came from, or the one we have to be at in twenty minutes, that we don't focus on what is happening now.

Yet life is made up of a constant series of "nows." The past was right now, just a second ago. The future will be right now in another second. If you don't make the most of the present, you will not have nearly as good a past, nor nearly as good a future as you could. If you constantly shortchange the present moment—the "now"—you will always be shortchanging your life.

Don't let that happen.

Instead, whenever your mind starts to wander, or you are out of focus, just ask yourself:

What is my A.M.? – Activity of the Moment
Who is my P.M.? – Person of the Moment

Everyone you come in contact with wants to be your Person of the Moment. When you choose to be with a person, fully focus on your chosen Person of the Moment and Activity of the Moment. When you do, you can make that person feel like a king or a queen! When you don't, you make that person feel like a peon.

How often have you been a party to this type of scenario? I'm busy working on my computer, preparing a proposal for my best customer. Susan walks into my office and has a question for me. I barely look up and reply to her inquiry with a "Yes? What is it?" As Susan proceeds with her question, I bob my head without ever making solid eye contact and continue to try and compose the proposal I was working on before she came in. I might mumble a "Yeah, uh-huh" here and a "Right" there, but clearly, I am not focusing on Susan.

I continue to shuffle through my notes, not really seeing them now. I still haven't looked directly at Susan. As she seems to finish, still clearly out of focus I say, "Uhh, I think so, Susan, if you think it makes sense."

When she is gone, what she has been talking about semi-sinks into my brain. I get up from my desk and trot down the hall after her, shouting, "Wait a minute, Susan. What were you saying? I don't think we can do that."

Now, in that situation, who was my Person of the Moment?

It certainly wasn't Susan. At best I was half listening to her. It was not my best customer, whom I was preparing the report for, because Susan's commentary kept interrupting my thoughts. It wasn't even me. It was nobody. I had no Person of the Moment. My time with Susan was not only unproductive, it was counterproductive. There is a high probability I gave her an inappropriate answer and set something in motion that would have to be reversed later. I made her feel like a lowly, unimportant person interrupting my busy day. I spent much more time as I chased her down the hall than I would have if I had changed my focus, changed my A.M. & P.M.

Instead, if I had just said, "Susan is this a quick question?" If her answer was, "Yes, I just need two minutes," then I would consciously tell myself, "For two minutes, my Activity of the Moment is to *listen,* and my Person of the Moment is *Susan.* And for two or three minutes, I would have stayed focused on that A.M. & P.M. I would have given her the full attention of my eyes, ears, and brain. I would have understood her question, given her an informed answer, and said a polite good-bye. Then I would have quickly refocused my brain to my previous A.M. & P.M.—the proposal and my client.

But what if Susan's response to "Is this a quick question?" was, "No. We need twenty to thirty minutes to outline next week's meeting." If you don't have twenty minutes right then, how do you tell Susan to go away in a nice way? Use A.M. & P.M.

"Susan, planning the meeting is important and, when we do it, I want to make sure I make it my Activity of the Moment and you and the rest of those attending my Persons of the Moment. I can't do that right now because I am committed to getting this proposal out to a client before lunch. Could we get together at one o'clock to outline the meeting?" Susan agrees. "Great. I'll see you in your office at one."

Before I turn my attention back to my pervious A.M. & P.M., what should I do? What do I have to do to ensure I don't let that commitment fall through the cracks along with my credibility?

Right. I need to WIN with "Meet with Susan" at 1:00 p.m. in my calendar. After I WIN, I can fully turn my mind back to my previous A.M. & P.M. I am free from having to keep mentally telling myself, "Don't forget about Susan." It's right in my calendar with a five-minute alarm set to prompt me.

Using A.M. & P.M. to focus your attention will make you a much more effective listener. In looking through a book my father owned, which was copyrighted in 1949, I found this quotation from Dorothy Dix, one of the most widely read newspaper columnists in the first part of the twentieth century: "The short cut to popularity is to lend everyone your ears, instead of giving them your tongue." The same is true in the twenty-first century.

I would add that you should not only listen with your ears but with your eyes and mind, as well. Make each person you come in contact with your Person of the Moment and listening fully to them your Activity of the Moment.

Learning the "F" Word

At our dinner table, when my loquacious daughter was about five, she was unusually quiet. I asked if she was OK. Her hesitant head nod prompted me to make her my person of the moment and to encourage her to tell us what she was thinking. Very timidly she said, "I learned the F-word at school today. I know it's a bad word and I won't ever say it. I shouldn't say it, should I?"

It was clear she wanted to verbalize more, so I responded, "No you shouldn't say it around others, but if you want to say it now, that's OK, and we can talk about it."

"Are you sure it's OK if I say it now?" she asked.

I nodded.

She paused and then whispered the word… "Fart."

Every time I think of this family moment, I marvel that my wife and I were able to restrain our abounding internal laughter and relief. Although my daughter hates when I bring it up, in addition to this being a big smile memory it's a good lesson. When you are listening, don't cut people off because you've jumped to an early conclusion of what is being said. Listen the person out, or you may very well go off in an unnecessary and more difficult direction.

Not focusing on your A.M. & P.M. can ruin a date, destroy a meeting, and make every encounter an insult. Focusing on them can multiply the value you and others receive from every encounter and every relationship. That is why the ability to focus is such a powerful personal and professional characteristic.

You may have heard the term "flow" or what athletes refer to as being in "the zone." This is a state of peak performance, where an individual outdoes himself and excellence almost becomes effortless.

Mihaly Csikszentmihalyi, a University of Chicago psychologist who created the term "flow," has spent decades researching this phenomenon. His studies include the accounts of hundreds of individuals from fields as different as rock climbing, engineering, management, athletics, even filing. These studies and others have shown that one of the key ways to enter flow is "to intentionally focus a sharp attention on the task at hand; a highly concentrated state is the essence of flow."[4]

Now, we all may not be able to nip the corner of the plate with a hundred mile-an-hour fastball or defeat Big Blue in a chess match, but we can greatly multiply our Achievement and Enjoyment in our professions, avocations, and relationships by using A.M. & P.M. to bring our attention into sharp focus.

Martha is a bank branch manager in Atlanta. When she was first promoted to this position, it overwhelmed her. With the constant demands of customers and employees she could never find the time

---

[4] Daniel Goleman, *Emotional Intelligence*

to complete the important paperwork required of her position, much less plan for creating improvements in the branch. "I felt like I was drowning." That changed when she started using A.M. & P.M.

Within six months, Martha went from struggling to survive to having one of the top branches in a very large bank. She credits the use of A.M. & P.M. as a key reason she rose to the top. "The customers always come first in our bank, so I never put them off. Instead, A.M. & P.M. helped me focus more effectively and quickly on their business needs."

"With my associates in the bank, I now had a polite way to explain that there were times when my A.M. needed to be paperwork or planning. I could politely ask them not to interrupt me during those times, except for emergencies. I set brief meeting times to see each of them once a day if needed and committed to making them my P.M when we did. They respected that, and I am now able to much more effectively focus on both the people and project sides of my job. A.M. & P.M. keeps my head above water."

Using A.M. & P.M. you will get more done, more quickly, and at the same time make everyone around you feel important. Be willing to switch your focus. Using A.M. & P.M. you will find that switching your focus is quick and easy to do. Tonight, when you are reading the paper and your spouse or roommate asks you a question, change your P.M. to that person and your A.M. to listening. Fold up the paper, look the person in the eye, and listen.

If it's important to you to finish what you are reading, make eye contact and say, "I'd like to hear about that. I'm in the middle of a good article right now. Let me finish, and then I can fully focus on you and what you are saying." Both of you will find that a lot more rewarding than trying to continue to read while you are thinking, *I wish he'd shut up.*

One of my clients is a major newspaper and media company. Two months after their training, we did a review session with their executive team, and they were discussing highlights from the training. The Senior Vice President said that her seven-year-old daughter had come to her, unsolicited, and said, "Mommy, I'm so glad you are spending extra time with me."

You know what the woman's highlight was? She was spending *less* time with her daughter! And she absolutely knew it. A major news cycle had broken, plus she had her regular job. She had never spent more time at work!

But when she was at home with her daughter, she was using A.M. & P.M. If she was in the kitchen cooking and her daughter was doing homework, she didn't count that as A.M. & P.M. time. But, if she said she would play a game with her daughter, for that ten or fifteen minutes, her A.M. was *play this game*. Her P.M. was *my daughter*.

In the past, she might make her move and then look at her laptop or check her email on her phone. Then she would return to the game saying something like, "Oh good move, honey," make her move, and be back glancing at her emails or interrupting for a call that came in.

Instead, when she was with her daughter, she was really with her daughter—no distractions, nothing popping into their A.M. & P.M. time that was more important. And her daughter's perception was: *Mommy is spending so much more time with me.*

So, when you are with someone, *really be with them*. Focus on your A.M. & P.M.

Everyone you come in contact with is a unique, individual part of your Big Picture. They want and need to be treated that way. Stay focused on your A.M. & P.M. with them. Each of you will get more done and have more fun doing it.

Quality Time – What Does it Mean?

The term "Quality Time" has been bandied about for a couple of decades. Most of us have heard the phrase, "It's not the amount of time you spend with someone, but the quality of the time." What does that mean? What is quality time?

I've gotten hundreds of answers to that question. "Quality time is meaningful time." "Quality time is focused time." "Quality time is when everyone involved gets something out of it." But what makes it meaningful? Focused on what?

Have you ever spent focused, one-on-one time with someone and still come away frustrated, knowing the connection you were hoping for just wasn't made? I experienced this at the lunches with my managers, where they were in a Play mode and I was in an Action mode.

What I have discovered from client discussions is that there is clearly no set definition for Quality Time. It changes daily, sometimes minute to minute and certainly from person to person.

Take the father who has a fifth-grade son making D's in school with a big test coming up on Tuesday. He is constantly playing with his son. The past weekend, he had taken him on an overnight camping trip. Sunday night, they watched the ball game on TV together. Monday night before the test, Dad comes home with a new video game and says, "How about breaking in this new game with me?" Is that quality time in that relationship on this particular Monday night? Probably not. Instead, the Action of helping his son hit the books, study hard, and succeed in learning would probably produce more valued, quality results for his son and their relationship.

What about the flip side of that equation? The mother who has pushed her daughter to study for the test for a week in advance. The young lady proved on Saturday and again on Sunday that she knows the material frontwards and backwards and is going a little brain dead from studying. Is another heavy review session in order? Probably not. More likely it's time for some pat-on-the-back Play time. "You've worked hard. Let's go to the yogurt shop and celebrate."

Whether at home or at work, with yourself or with others, you need to vary your time between Think, Act and Play. To get the most "quality" out of your time with another person, determine whether you should spend Think, Act, or Play time with that individual. When you do use TAP to vary how you spend your time in a relationship, you can make your time and that relationship more valuable than you may have realized was possible.

You create valuable quality time by
predetermining
which TAP function to emphasize in the relationship.
When you do, focus on your A.M. & P.M.

Practice TAP, WIN, and AM. & P.M. on a daily basis until they become habits and you will routinely create more valuable time with each important person in your life.

Summary

- If you constantly shortchange the present moment—the "now"—you will always be shortchanging your life.
- A.M. & P.M. helps you capture the value of a present moment and improve your active listening skills.
- Remember to focus on your "Activity of the Moment" and "Person of the Moment."
- When you do, you make those around you feel more valued, improve your relationships, and get more done.

Your Emotional Management Tool

Happiness Meter – Tool # 5

"Emotional aptitude is a meta-ability, determining how well we can use whatever other skills we have, including raw intellect."
— Daniel Goleman

How do we know when we successfully TAP into someone? Or how do we know when we are moving forward on our Big Picture goals? What tells us that we are succeeding in achieving balance in all parts of our lives?

As humans, what is our feedback mechanism?

When things are going well in our lives, we describe ourselves as being happy. On the opposite side, when the pieces of our life are in a jumble, or when we're frustrated and frowning a lot, we are unhappy.

These emotions have a powerful impact on our lives. Research in "quick reaction" situations shows that the emotional part of our brain kicks in a moment or two before our rational thinking process. If we don't have a way to check those emotions, we may make ill-informed decisions or take rash actions.[5] This simple fact brings us to the last tool in the TAP process.

Each of us has a built-in emotional feedback meter. It's standard equipment at birth. I call it your Happiness Meter˚. The visual that follows represents that emotional feedback system we all have inside of us.

_____

[5] Daniel Goleman, Emotional Intelligence

Don't take this little meter lightly. When I lead trainings with top executives, I present them with a physical Happiness Meter. Those meters sit on some of the top executive desks in this country.

As one example, Bob is a senior partner at one of the top law firms in the Eastern United States. He is a trusted advisor to some of the world's most financially successful entrepreneurs and business leaders. He serves on the boards of several major institutions, including a major league baseball organization.

On a visit to Bob's office you would find his Happiness Meter sitting on his desk. After every partners' meeting, he would reset it, at least in his mind. If he mentally jammed it to the left, frowny side, it made him stop and think why he was so dissatisfied. "The flow of this meeting was very confusing. I don't like this new format. I'm going to make a note to rearrange it for next week's meeting." If he was pleased and his meter reading was far on the right side, he might respond, "That junior partner made an excellent presentation today. I'm going to take him to lunch, pat him on the back, and learn a little more about him."

A couple of years ago, his law firm moved its offices. Bob called me shortly after the move and informed me that his Happiness Meter had been lost in the move and that he would like another one. In his deliberate and friendly-style, he said, "Jim, I've got two of the best baseball tickets you will ever see if you can get me another one of those Happiness Meters."

My immediate response was, "Absolutely. In fact, if you've got four of those tickets, I'm sure I could find you a backup meter." I have never had better seats at major league game.

The Happiness Meter is not something Bob needs to have on his desk. Long before I met him, he had earned a well-deserved reputation for having exceptional people and professional skills. I have been privileged to benefit and learn from those skills. The meter on his desk just serves as a little reminder for him to recognize and respond quickly to his feelings about people and events. The ability to do this is very valuable to our life success.

Daniel Goleman in his best-selling book, *Emotional Intelligence*, documents the "crucial role of feeling in navigating the endless stream of life's personal decisions."[6] Goleman points out that while strong emotions can cause havoc in reasoning, the lack of awareness of emotions can be equally hazardous. Emotional self-awareness is the "building block" for being able to shake off a bad mood and reason clearly.

The Happiness Meter is an emotional self-awareness tool. It is a fun way of taking a serious look at life.

You should take your Happiness Meter reading and respond to it every day in each quadrant of your life. Ask yourself, "What is my overall Happiness Meter reading in my entire life right now?" Draw in an arrow below or mentally set your current reading.

---

[6] Daniel Goleman, Emotional Intelligence, p. 53

As important as understanding where you would place yourself on the Happiness Meter is knowing where that reading is coming from. How you feel about your life at a given moment comes from the sum of its respective parts.

What are your current readings in each quadrant of your life? Draw them in or set them mentally now.

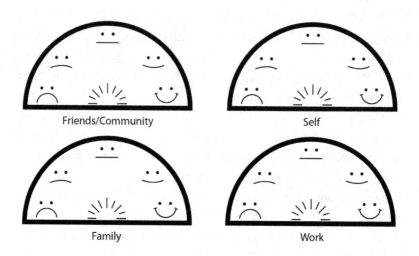

You may have discovered in doing this that a negative reading in one area of your life can have a disproportional effect on all the others. The opposite is also true. A strong positive reading in one area can have a disproportionately positive impact on the other areas. For example, a very positive reading in the self-area, because of excellent physical health, can reflect itself in much more confidence and success on the job.

Where do each of your quadrant readings come from? They originate primarily from individual relationship readings. What is your current reading with your spouse, your best friend, your parents? Where is your Happiness Meter reading with each of your children, or your new customer, or your boss, or yourself right now? If you are not especially happy with a reading, you should TAP into that person.

After you do this, check your Happiness Meter to see how you feel about the results.

When you TAP into yourself, recognize that you choose which side of the meter you are going to live on. In today's world, you should: *Reject the left side of the Happiness Meter as an acceptable, normal state. It is your responsibility to live your life on the right side of the Happiness Meter.*

You may have been taught or concluded that the left, frowny side of the meter is the rule. You may have heard that "Happiness is a fleeting thing, so you had better grab every little bit of it that comes along." That's bull!

Happiness is *not* a fleeting thing, not in the advanced or advancing country I suspect you live in if you are reading this book. If you are living in a war-torn, disease-stricken, third-world country, then maybe the left side would be the everyday rule. But in a world that offers up so many wonderful potential Achievements and Enjoyments to us every day, the left side should be the exception and not the rule.

Does this mean you will always be happy? Or that every day is going to be a walk in the park? No. Tragic things are going to happen in everyone's life. For most of us, however, real tragedies are the exception. Every day, we have the greatest opportunity in history to achieve and enjoy. We should expect to live the vast majority of our days on the right side of our Happiness Meter.

How important is understanding your emotions and training your brain to live on the right side of the Happiness Meter? Your life could depend on it.

Studies of medical students conducted at Duke University by Dr. Redford Williams found that those physicians who scored highest on a test of hostility while still in medical school were seven times as likely to have died by the age of fifty as were those with low hostility scores.

"Training your brain" to live on the positive side is critical to both your Achievement and your Enjoyment. Positive emotions release chemicals that help your brain think more flexibly and deeply about both problems and opportunities. Bad moods, conversely, make it more likely for chemicals to constrict our brains, generating fear and often resulting in no decision or overly cautious ones. Such noxious emotions risk our health as much as smoking two packs a day.

So, don't be stoic. Your emotions tell you important things. Your Achievement and Enjoyment, and your life itself, depend on them. Read and respond to them quickly with the important individuals in every area of your life. Use your emotions to catch negative trends before they build into disaster, or to spot positive trends so you can keep doing what is working.

One of the problems in doing this is reading our own emotions. They aren't visible to the naked eye and can be hard for us to understand, especially in times of frustration or busyness. The Happiness Meter is a way to remind yourself not to disregard your emotions and to manifest them in a more tangible way. It can help you capture and slow them down, so you can respond calmly and rationally.

You might be thinking, "It may be nice to say you are going to reject the left side and live on the right side, but how do you do it? How do you consistently stay happy in life?"

The first thing to realize is that your Happiness Meter (your emotions) will not tell you how! Your Happiness Meter is only a gauge or indicator of the results of your choices. Emotions should *not* be used as the primary basis for *making* choices. They will not tell you how to get on or stay on the right course.

The Happiness Meter and your corresponding emotions are like a depth finder on a boat. They will tell you whether you are in the deep-blue waters of happiness or in the shallows of life. But emotions will not tell you how you got there, how to stay there, or how to change course.

The same could be said for the thermometer. It will tell you whether you have a fever, whether you are sick or well, but you can't ask the thermometer how to get better and expect an answer. Neither can you expect an answer from your emotions on how to keep your life good or make it better.

In the 1960s, the catch phrase was, "Do whatever makes you happy, man." Well, that tells you absolutely nothing. If you knew what would make you happy just by feeling it, there would be no question in the first place.

A friend and client once told me, "Decisions based on emotions were the ruination of a big part of my early life." Emotions are a very dangerous basis for making important decisions. If you want to choose the movie you are going to see tonight because you "feel" like a comedy, that's great, have a ball. That is not a major life decision. But don't quit a job, end a valued relationship, or make any important life decision only because you feel like it.

If you do, you will emotionally ricochet through life, bouncing from feeling good to feeling bad, with no real clue as to how to stay on the feeling-good track. Respond to your emotions as a critical life measurement, both as an Enjoyment meter and as an early warning system. But remember too that: *Happiness is a consequence of your good choices and not the basis for making them.*

Instead, the basis for making good choices is using reasoning to continuously reconnect you to your Achievement and Enjoyment goals. TAP will accomplish that connection with the important individuals in your life. The review on the next few pages will solidify that process for you and help it become a part of your daily interactions.

The TAP Summary

1. Put one Face on your Balance Watch.
2. Determine whether you've been Thinking, Acting, or Playing enough in this relationship.
3. Decide if that's OK in light of your goals and Happiness Meter reading.
4. Pre-determine which TAP Function to emphasize in this relationship now.
5. Choose the specific alternative to improve your Thinking, Action, or Playing, and WIN with it in your daily calendar.

6. Focus on your A.M. & P.M. to Achieve and Enjoy those choices fully.

7. Check your Happiness Meter regularly with each important person in your Big Picture to evaluate the success of your TAP choices.

Take thirty seconds now and mentally walk through this simple process shown visually on the next page. Starting by putting a face on the Watch, ask yourself the TAP questions, then mentally flow through the rest of the process.

The TAP Process

Start Here

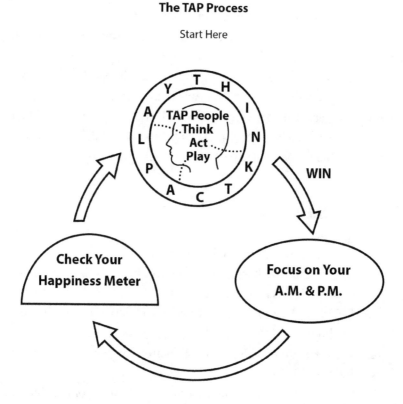

Starting at the top, you mentally put a face on the Watch and asked yourself three TAP questions.

Have I been:

- Thinking enough about this person?
- Acting enough with this person?
- Playing enough with this person?

"Is that OK?" If your answers were not OK, then you would WIN with the specific Thinking, Action, or Play item in your calendar.

When it comes time to be with that person, focus on your chosen Activity of the Moment and make that individual your Person of the Moment. Afterward, check your Happiness Meter to determine how things went. If they went especially well, you may move on to another person, or WIN with a time to do a similar thing again with that individual.

If you do not feel good about the results, then you may need to TAP into that individual in a different way, such as emphasizing Action instead of Play. If you choose Think as your first TAP, block "Think time" with a WIN in your calendar. In Part 3 we will cover a supercharger technique for all your think time.

The three TAP Functions are like the electrons, neutrons, and protons of relationships. Thinking, Acting and Playing are the three life essentials in every relationship. By using TAP, you can instantaneously recombine those essentials to create amazing results!

Create those amazing results in different ways, every day, with all the important people in your life. TAP into them regularly to help keep your Happiness Meter on the right side of life.

Summary

- Emotional self-awareness is the building block for making reasoned choices and enjoying life.
- The Happiness Meter® is a tool that manifests emotions in a more tangible way, so you can recognize them and then respond rationally.
- Ask yourself, "What is my overall Happiness Meter reading in each quadrant and across my entire life right now?" Train your brain to live on the positive side!
- Being aware of your emotions helps you understand the *results* of your choices. To make new choices, use the TAP reasoning tool to determine what actions to take next.

Changing Your Life Emphasis for More Value & Balance

Emphasis Settings – Tool #6

"It is a mistake to build your whole life around one quadrant of your Big Picture."
— Jim Bird

For each of us, there are certain quadrants of our Big Picture where we want and need to spend more time because we have more pieces to deal with in that part of our life picture. A single parent with young children will probably spend more time in the Family Quadrant than a single individual with no children. Most of us invest more time in the Work Quadrant of our lives than in some other sections. This is appropriate. The Work Quadrant provides the financial means to pay for life's necessities, as well as the array of Achievement and Enjoyment opportunities in the other areas of your Big Picture.

Even though one area may require more time, it is a mistake to build your whole life around just one quadrant of your Big Picture. The key to living your life successfully and keeping your Happiness Meter on the right side, is to get the most out of the time you spend in each quadrant, even if it is limited. This is harder to do when you are adding pieces that don't connect well with your life objectives or neglecting the ones that will. Emphasis settings trigger your attention to a given quadrant and help ensure that your life picture comes together the way you want it to.

This is important. If one or more of our life quadrants is in a jumble, then at best our lives are less fulfilling than they could be. At worst, life could become tragic. I can quote you dire stories from the *Wall Street Journal, People, The New York Times*, local newspapers, and client experiences, of great employees and great leaders who became liabilities to their organizations because they were unable to manage and enjoy the non-work sides of their lives. These were individuals who built their entire lives around work.

In the first company I co-founded, we had promoted a hard-working and capable manager to the role of vice president. He stayed late almost every night. When I would be leaving the office at seven or eight o'clock, I would usually say, "Go home, Bill. Don't burn yourself out here. Get some time with your wife and family."

His response was always, "I've just got a few more things to finish up."

As I drove home, I remember thinking, *I tried to get him out of there, but...I sure am getting my money's worth out of that guy.*

Because over the years he continued to do a good job, we delegated more and more to him until he was running the largest portion of our firm. I had stopped looking over his shoulder closely and did not realize how both his family life and his own health had deteriorated. He was building his whole life around his Work Quadrant. As the stresses external to work increased, they began to impact his dealings with the people in our business. The resultant damage was major, both to our bottom line and Bill's career with our company. I am convinced these very negative outcomes would have been avoided if Bill had been able to get more value from and keep more balance within all the quadrants of his life.

That experience further drove home work-life balance as an essential component not only of individual wellness and fulfillment but also of organizational performance and leadership succession.

This overemphasis on one quadrant is not limited to the work area alone. Early in our marriage, my wife Vikki and I became friends with a woman named Joan. I enjoyed Joan from the moment I met her because she had an extremely positive and upbeat outlook on life. She worked to help put her husband through college. After he graduated and got a good-paying professional position, she quit work. Shortly thereafter, she became the proud mom of a handsome son.

From that point on, Joan focused her life almost exclusively around the Family Quadrant, specifically her husband and son. She didn't keep up or add to any of her professional skills. She lost touch with her friends. She gained weight. Her clear intellectual curiosity about the world seemed to wane. After twelve years of devoting herself to her small family, her husband filed for divorce.

Joan was crushed. It was as if her whole world had collapsed, and in many ways, it had because she had built her whole life around that quadrant. For a couple of years, her upbeat outlook on life retreated to the recesses of her being and sadness became a way of life for her.

Then one Saturday, I picked up the phone at our house, and it was Joan. She sounded like her old self. Through the phone she projected a joy of living; a delightfully contagious sense of happiness. I said, "Joan, what's happening?"

She said, "Oh, Jim, I just got back from Prague, Czechoslovakia and it was so wonderful." She went on to describe Prague and its people, buildings, and restaurants with delight in every word. Her enthusiasm put Prague on my list of must-see cities.

Because of this joyous description, I casually remarked, "It's a great big wonderful world out there, isn't it, Joan?"

There was a moment of silence in response before Joan, in a subdued tone, said, "Yes, Jim, and I never knew that before."

Well, it was always a great, big, wonderful world out there. Joan just had not stayed in touch with it; stayed connected to the relationships and self-building interests and experiences that make all of us more rich and vibrant individuals. She now makes it a point to stay connected to all her life quadrants and in doing so benefits not only herself but all those around her.

Similarly, when each of us stay in balance with connections to our friends, work, and ourselves, our families benefit too. We are healthier and more complete physically and mentally. As a result, we are better parents, spouses, friends, and romantic partners to those we care most deeply about.

The TAP Process can easily keep you connected to the important individual relationships in all four areas of your life. But there are some very important facts you need to recognize about balancing your time between different people and different activities.

The proper balance for you will never be an equal balance.
Your proper balance will always change.
You stay in balance by getting out of balance.

Now pay special attention to that last, seemingly contradictory statement: "You stay in balance by getting out of balance."

Staying in balance is like steering a boat. Imagine you are captaining a small skiff from the shore to a lighthouse that is two miles out to sea. You start the engine, pull the anchor, put the motor in gear, and aim the bow directly at the lighthouse. Grasping the steering wheel tightly, you accelerate toward your destination. If you continue to firmly hold the wheel in the direction you have started, without making any adjustment left or right, will you arrive at the lighthouse?

Certainly not. What happens? As you grip the wheel you soon find that the lighthouse is way off to your left, so you steer left. Within a few minutes, the lighthouse probably ends up ahead on your right, so you steer right. You continue this pattern of left and right adjustment until you get to the light house. You stayed on course by getting off course. The same is true in life. You stay in balance by getting out of balance.

Over time you can get much better at captaining your craft and make smaller adjustments sooner, before getting too far off course. But for the rest of your life you will be making those adjustments. Your proper balance will always be changing. You will stay in balance by getting out of balance.

To keep your balance and sense of well-being you must remember:

You can't be all things to all people at the same time.
You can't even be equal things to all people at the same time.

You have to recognize and accept these two simple facts to reduce much of the unnecessary stress and guilt in life. Emphasis Settings are very helpful in doing that.

Emphasis Settings – Balance Within and Between Your Life Quadrants

Your Emphasis Setting is what you want or need to spend the bulk of your time or energy on right now. It is your current focal point. It determines your mental availability for particular projects or people.

Recognizing, choosing, and communicating your Emphasis Settings makes sorting through your choices much easier, enables others to offer encouragement and support, and helps you avoid unnecessary stress and guilt.

Here are the very simple steps to determine your Emphasis Setting, illustrated in a representative example from Lisa, a working mom who decided to change her Emphasis.

Lisa's Emphasis Settings

(Example)

1. Circle one TAP Function in each Quadrant as Your Emphasis Setting in that area right now:

Work	T(A)P
Family	T(A)P
Friends	T A(P)
Self	(T)A P

2. Circle the one Quadrant above that is your CURRENT overall Emphasis

⟨Work	T(A)P⟩
Family	T(A)P
Friends	T A(P)
Self	(T)A P

3. Is that OK? Yes /(No)

4. If not, what quadrant would you like to be your Emphasis moving forward, and what TAP function within that quadrant would you emphasize?

Work	T(A)P
Family	T(A)P
Friends	T A(P)
⟨Self	T(A)P⟩

5. Why?

Major job responsibilities completed. Gained weight; energy level down. It is important to my job, my family, and me to stay healthy.

6. Have you communicated your overall Emphasis Setting and the reasons for it to all the important people in your life?   Yes /(No)

Not yet. WIN for tonight.

In Section 1, Lisa circled "A" for the Work Quadrant because she had been emphasizing Action at work. She had recently assumed a new role and there was a great deal to do in both her old and new job during the transition. She had been emphasizing Action with her family, taking care of the necessary things with her husband and household while she put in a lot of time at work. Play had been her emphasis with friends when she saw them. In the Self quadrant, she had been Thinking about her health and that it needed some attention.

Her response to Section 2 was to circle the entire work quadrant as having been her overall life emphasis recently because of the demands of her job transition.

Lisa's answer to "Is that OK?" was "No." She felt a need to reconnect with her family and herself. In particular she wanted to get on an exercise program to lose a little weight and increase her energy level.

In Section 4 she elected to change the TAP emphasis within two of her life quadrants. She chose to switch her family emphasis to Play, taking a little fun time with her husband. She wrote in her calendar to schedule a "Date" with him. In the Self area, she switched her emphasis to Act from Think. She wanted to start back on her exercise program and stick to it. For her it was important to both her physical and mental health.

Most importantly she changed her overall Emphasis Setting from Work Action to Self Action. This change did not mean she intended to stop going to work or stop doing her job in anything but a superior way. Changing her emphasis to Self simply meant that for a few of weeks when faced with either working late or getting her exercise in, she was going to choose to exercise most of the time. She chose to focus on herself, because it was the area where she had gotten most out of balance...off her desired course.

In response to Question 5, "Why?" Lisa wrote the reason for this change of emphasis.

By writing the reason down, it makes it pass through your brain, down through your fingers and onto paper, creating more permanent synaptic connections in your brain than if you just thought about it. The result is a more solid ongoing memory fix on the "why," and therefore more motivation to follow through.

Prompted by Question 6, she entered a WIN for that evening to discuss her emphasis change with her husband and ask for his help in encouraging her to exercise in the evenings. With his support, Lisa was successful in mentally emphasizing and committing to her exercise program as a priority for several weeks. Once she got back into the habit of regularly exercising, she was able to continue with her workouts without making it her primary mental setting, at least for a while.

All of us steering through life need to routinely make course adjustments within and between our quadrants. Emphasis settings make that happen sooner rather than later.

There will be times when you evaluate your Emphasis Settings and determine not to switch your overall emphasis between quadrants at all. But you may want to change your TAP emphasis within a quadrant. Lisa's decision to move from Action to Play in the family quadrant is an example of this.

Speaking of Play, let me mention vacations here. To recharge and have the most fun on your vacations, you must truly switch your quadrant emphasis away from work and change your TAP emphasis to Play. Do not walk around the office making sure everyone has your cell number saying, "Call me if you need anything at all." Say just the opposite. Give one person your number and say, "Please do not call me unless it is an absolute emergency. This is Play time that I've set aside for my family/friends/self, and I want to stay focused on that." Ideally leave your laptop at home and limit or avoid checking work-emails on your phone.

OK, your turn. This is an easy exercise. Take up to three minutes to determine your current and desired Emphasis Settings on the following page or download and print Emphasis Setting worksheets here: worklifebalance.com/worksheets.

Emphasis Setting

1. Circle one TAP Function in each Quadrant as your Emphasis setting in that area right now:

Work	T A P
Family	T A P
Friends	T A P
Self	T A P

2. Circle the one Quadrant above that is your overall Emphasis setting.

3. Is that OK?   Yes / No

4. If not, what would you like your Emphasis to be now?

Work	T A P
Family	T A P
Friends	T A P
Self	T A P

5. Why?

_____

_____

_____

_____

6. Have you communicated your overall Emphasis setting and the reasons for it to all the important people in your life?

Yes / No

Whether you changed your Emphasis Setting or left it the same, ask yourself whether you have communicated this fact to the important people in your life. This is an extremely valuable step, which allows them to offer you encouragement and support, as well as eliminate stress and guilt.

In the early stages of building my current organization, my emphasis was generally Work and Action. I took the time to communicate this to my wife Vikki and our young daughters, Amanda and Kelly. We discussed the importance of our new company's success to all of our futures. This understanding helped. If I was working on a client presentation in the evening and had to say no to a request from Kelly to shoot basketball, it didn't make her happy, but she understood why.

That understanding reflected itself in many small ways. One of the most important paybacks I received was in the form of sticky notes from my daughters. In training, I use a lightweight black music stand to hold my course workbook. Periodically I would discover yellow sticky notes with smiley faces and hearts and wonderful messages stuck inside the notebook. "#1 Dad. We're behind you 100%. Love, Kelly." "Good luck on whatever you are doing as you read this. You're great. Amanda." It is hard not to be motivated to do a great job when you have that kind of reinforcement.

Emphasis Settings help you realize that you can be there for all the important people in your life, just not all at the same time. When others know and understand your Emphasis Settings, they are better prepared to assist and support you. They can also make it easier for you to choose how to allot your time.

Check your settings regularly. Be willing to change them for a day, a weekend, or for several weeks or months. Select and balance Thinking, Acting, *and* Playing in every quadrant. When you do, more daily Achievement and Enjoyment will become a routine way of living.

Summary

- A happy life is one where you get the most out of the time you spend in each quadrant, even if it is limited.
- Emphasis Settings help you prioritize where and how you want to spend the bulk of your time and energy.
- Your settings and balance will never be equal, and will always be changing.
- Check in on your Emphasis Settings regularly. Communicate them to your friends and family to avoid unnecessary guilt, and so they can better support you.

PART THREE

Achieving More In Life and Work

Supercharge Your Thinking

List & Prioritize – Tool #7

"Organizing is what you do before you do something, so that when you do it, it is not all mixed up."

A. A. Milne

By the end of this chapter you will possess an extremely simple technique that will multiply the quality and speed of your decision making. It will supercharge your brain, replacing worry with powerfully reasoned results.

When grappling with issues and decisions, the most active part of your reasoning brain is your working memory. This is a very specific part of the brain that has a surprisingly limited storage capacity. The average individual can hold only seven pieces of simple information in his working memory at time.[7] Even if you are 50% above average, you would be limited to ten.

When you try to think through a subject of any complexity in your head, you are greatly restricting your opportunities for a successful outcome. It's as if you were trying to put a puzzle together with your eyes closed. You can't see and remember all the pieces, so you may never find the one that fits best, or at all.

---

[7] George A. Miller, "The Magical Number Seven, Plus or Minus Two: Some Limits on Our Capacity for Processing Information" *Psychological Review*, 1956, Princeton University's Department of Psychology.

Wouldn't it be nice, when thinking through a major decision, to have all the relevant pieces to the decision laid out in front of you? Then you could see them all clearly, sort them, rearrange them, and connect them in the most effective way.

Fortunately, there is such a quick and easy way to supercharge your working memory and at least double your ability to see the pieces and arrive quickly at a positive solution. Whenever you need to plan a meeting, a vacation, talking points, or think through any decision, supercharge your reasoning brain with this simple method.

The *List and Prioritize* Method

Start by focusing on one opportunity, problem, communication, or issue you've been stewing about. Take out a piece of paper or open a spreadsheet and just start listing what you might do to solve it. Write down whatever comes to your mind no matter how wild or crazy it may seem.

After you have made the list, sort through the pieces by prioritizing them as either A, B, or C. Then just focus on the A's and tag them 1,2,3,4, etc. by their priority order. Write at least your A1 in your calendar on the day you will do it. Now you are on your way.

In summary, here are the simple steps. <u>Each one is critical</u> to very quick and effective thinking.

1. List as many options as you can to address an objective or issue, or to draft communications.
2. Prioritize each option as an A, B, or C.
3. Prioritize each "A" option as A_1, A_2, A_3, etc.
4. WIN – Write It Now in your calendar on the day you will execute or start your priority.

Although most of us are generally aware of the power of writing down information to improve your reasoning, its power is consistently overlooked. Simply writing down the information you are grappling with, or that you need to prioritize, exponentially increases the effectiveness of your thinking. It allows you to multiply the number of things your working memory could otherwise effectively deal with. It is also a very enjoyable way of thinking. Part of the fun is that there are no rights or wrongs when you begin listing the possibilities. Write down whatever comes to your mind no matter how wild it may seem. Once you complete your list, then you can prioritize it and determine what to focus on.

One Sunday my wife commented on her supercharged list for the weekend. "I got so much done this weekend and it wouldn't have happened without my prioritized list. Otherwise, what I end up doing is pondering about what I could do and it's overwhelming. I don't know where to start. Before I know it, it's Sunday afternoon and I've gotten next to nothing done. I took three minutes on Friday to write the possibilities down, prioritized them, and Saturday morning I was off and running." Her list looked like this:

A1 – *Clean out bathroom closet – Sunday*

A2 – *Plant vegetable garden – Start Saturday*

A3 – *Hang new pictures in bedroom – Sunday if time*

B1 – *Finish knitting scarf – Sunday if time*

Simple, easy, quick, and satisfying.

Below is a more detailed example from one of my clients for her work quadrant. Claire had been frustrated with the effectiveness of the communications in her company and her role in improving them. She used List & Prioritize to quickly think through options she had to improve her impact on team communication and coordination at work.

1. **List as many options as you can to...**
   "Better my impact on improving communications within the company."
     Better prepare for staff meetings
     Greet everyone w/smile

Have lunch w/Jill – missed B-day
Train on new software system
Have lunch with out of town managers when in office
WIN with staff meeting follow through

2. **Prioritize each option as an A, B or C.**
    A   *Better prepare for staff meetings*
    A   *Greet everyone w/smile*
    A   *Have lunch w/Jill – missed B-day*
    B   *Train on new software system*
    B   *Have lunch with out of town managers when in office*
    A   *WIN with staff meeting follow through*

3. **Prioritize each A option as A1, A2, A3, etc.**
    A1 *Better prepare for staff meetings*
    A3 *Greet everyone w/smile*
    A4 *Have lunch w/Jill – missed B-day*
    B   *Train on new software system*
    B   *Have lunch with out of town managers when in office*
    A2 *WIN with staff meeting follow through*

4. **WIN - Write at least your A1 in your calendar now.**

When Claire completed the List & Prioritize process, she concluded that her A1 item to improve her team's coordination and communication was to better prepare herself for the weekly staff meetings. The department's staff meeting was Monday morning. She wrote in her calendar every Friday for a month to *prepare for staff meeting.* Her A2 item was to WIN with her follow-through items from those staff meetings. There had been lots of talk, but little action from these meetings. She wanted to correct that from her end. She wrote down on four consecutive Mondays in her calendar to "WIN from Staff Meeting."

Her A3 was greet everyone with a smile. With the pressure and changes she had been going through at work she thought she had gotten a little sour. To remind herself she put a smiley face in her calendar every other day for a month. Her A4 item served both her friendship with Jill and their professional relationship. She enjoyed Jill and wanted to celebrate her birthday for fun. She wrote in her calendar on the following Monday to ask Jill to lunch.

Claire completed these Thinking steps in less than five minutes. When you use List & Prioritize, you multiply the capabilities of your working memory. As a result, good thinking doesn't take long. Claire also followed through on all of these things, immediately improving her effectiveness. As a result, her Enjoyment levels on her job increased, as did those of her team.

Shorter, More Effective Meetings

Claire told me she also supercharged her meeting preparation and delivery time. When she was planning for the meeting, she used the List & Prioritize method to identify...

- The three most important things she needed to say at each meeting
- The three most important things she needed to find out

"With my top three say and ask items thought through ahead of time, when I'm asked at the meeting, 'what do you think?', I can say, "I think that (1, 2, 3)... and I need to know (1) from you John, (2) from you Sue, and approval of (3) from you Carol." Instead of ten to fifteen minutes of rambling through her ideas and questions, Claire now makes her top points and gathers the input she needs in a couple of minutes. By doing this religiously, she has created a great reputation for herself as a prepared and on-top-of-things player. She also set an example and expectation that caught on with others. In the meetings she attends there is now less "Thinking by talking out loud" during the meeting because more thinking and preparation has been done before the meeting.

We have found that clients who implement this top three "ask" and "tell" preparation requirement for all meetings consistently reduce their meeting times, often by more than 50 percent.

Remember, when you stew over things, you are not thinking. Thinking is "reasoning toward a conclusion." Stewing is "fretting, fuming, worrying." When you stew too long, you dry up, you lose all your mental juices, your brain seems to shrivel. STOP! Start thinking by writing it down.

Now we are going to apply this List & Prioritize approach to identify and implement the most important projects in your life right now.

Summary

- The average individual retains only seven pieces of information in the working memory at a time.
- List & Prioritize supercharges your working memory by allowing you to identify, see, sort, and arrive at reasoned solutions more quickly.
- Once you list your options, prioritize them A,B,C and 1,2,3, etc. and then WIN the top priorities in your calendar on the day you intend to do them.
- Ahead of meetings, identifying your three "ask" and "tell" talking points can greatly improve your effectiveness.

Identifying & Completing Your Most Important Projects

PATH – Tool #8

"Your life will be no better than the plans you make,
and the action you take."
— Alfred Armand Montapert

TAP, WIN, and A.M. & P.M. enrich the moments, days, and decades you share with people. But to accomplish your goals of Achievement and Enjoyment you need more than just good relationships with people. You also need a roof over your head, food on the table, transportation, a job, an income. You need to focus on the important things you need and want and set a course that enables you to accomplish them. The PATH method for completing projects helps you set the course to get there.

PATH helps you quickly determine the most important projects and activities that will turn your everyday goals of Achievement and Enjoyment into reality by leveraging the List & Prioritize method covered in the previous chapter.

There are four simple elements to successfully completing a PATH to the things you want.

The PATH Method

P = Project	Select the *Project*
A = Activities	Determine the *Activities* to complete it
T = Time	Pick a *Time* for the first Activity and WIN
H = Harvest	Complete the Activity and *Harvest* the benefits

The individual PATHs that follow are representative of thousands of real people producing life-changing Achievements by investing *minutes* to make a PATH. The biggest stumbling block in this process is getting a pen and paper or spreadsheet in front of you before you begin. We've made that easy by giving you a page in this book to do your PATH. Let's start with a personal example in the family quadrant to show you how it works.

The PATH Method

Projects **(P)** – Determine the projects that help you accomplish your Family quadrant goal by using the List & Prioritize method.

1. List as many Family project options as you can
2. Prioritize each option as an A, B, or C.
3. Prioritize each "A" option as A_1, A_2, A_3, etc.

Below are the Projects I listed that came to mind in my family quadrant. The list looked like this:

Projects – Family Quadrant

Rank	Projects
	Refinance house
	Plan Father's birthday/family reunion
	College preferences for Kelly
	Clean out storage area
	Plan fishing trip with brothers

Then I prioritized them A, B, and C (no D's)

	Projects – Family Quadrant	
Rank	Projects
B	Refinance house
A	Plan Father's birthday/family reunion
A	College preferences for Kelly
C	Clean out storage area
A	Plan fishing trip with brothers

As you can see, "clean out the storage area" quickly became a C. It still is. Next, I refined the list by prioritizing the A's as 1,2,3, etc.

	Projects – Family Quadrant	
Rank	Projects
B	Refinance house
A2	Plan Father's birthday/family reunion
A1	**College preferences for Kelly**
C	Clean out storage area
A3	Plan fishing trip with brothers

My A1, most important project in the Family quadrant was to help my daughter Kelly determine her college preference and prepare. That completed the P part of PATH, which brought me to the **A** in PATH, prioritizing the **Activities** to complete my chosen project.

Activities (A) - Choose the specific Activities that help you complete your chosen projects by using the List and Prioritize Method.

The purpose here is to sort down from the bigger project level to a specific enough Activity that you can act on it. I took a separate sheet of paper, wrote my A1 Project at the top and listed all the Activities I could think of. I ended up with a fairly long list:

Family Quadrant
A1 Project – College Plan for Kelly

Rank	Activities
	Discuss her interests and possible majors
	Discuss types of colleges (big, small, sports oriented)
	Make up a list of possible choices with her
	Pick 2 – 3 to visit this summer
	Check out entrance requirements from college book
	Get Kelly to Prioritize top 5
	Schedule SAT prep course for August/September
	Visit colleges
	Begin application process
	Set time with Kelly to review. Ask her what dates work.

The next thing to do was to prioritize the list A, B, C.

Family Quadrant
A1 Project – College Plan for Kelly

Rank	Activities
A	Discuss her interests and possible majors
A	Discuss types of colleges (big, small, sports oriented)
A	Make up a list of possible choices with her
A	Pick 2 – 3 to visit this summer
A	Check out entrance requirements from college book
A	Get Kelly to Prioritize top 5
A	Schedule SAT prep course for August/September
A	Visit colleges
A	Begin application process
A	Set time with Kelly to review. Ask her what dates work.

They all became A's. What's the next step? Right. Prioritize each A as an A1, A2, A3…and so on.

Family Quadrant
A1 Project – College Plan for Kelly

Rank	Activities
A3	Discuss her interests and possible majors
A2	Discuss types of colleges (big, small, sports oriented)
A4	Make up a list of possible choices with her
A7	Pick 2 – 3 to visit this summer
A5	Check out entrance requirements from college book
A6	Get Kelly to Prioritize top 5
A8	Schedule SAT prep course for August/September
A9	Visit colleges
A10	Begin application process
A1	Set time with Kelly to review. Ask her what dates work.

My A1 became the last item listed, to set a time with Kelly to go over this PATH. Now the **T** in PATH stands for **Time.** This brings us right back to WIN (Write It Now).

Time (T) – WIN in your calendar the specific day you will start and expect to complete each Activity that you can schedule now.

You must make a connection in time when you will do what you have decided. If you do not, you have just wasted your time and mental energy thinking through the subject. I decided to do my A1 on the evening of April 19. I took out my calendar and got a WIN on that evening to "Agree with Kelly on a time to go over this college PATH together."

She agreed on April 21 for our discussion, where we covered a number of the top A's and set WINs for most of the remaining activities on the list. The Time step of PATH is the most critical part of the process. To successfully complete a PATH you need to set a time and WIN in your calendar on the day you will start or complete each activity.

Which then brings you to the H in PATH, which stands for Harvest.

Harvest (H) - Go out and *Harvest* the new pieces to add to your Big Picture and be sure to focus on your:

A.M. - Activity of the Moment

&

P.M. - Person of the Moment

Harvesting is where you reap the rewards and benefits of the PATH you have made. It delivers the satisfaction of follow-through and a sense of accomplishment. When you are Harvesting on your A1 PATH Project, you are doing the most important Activity on your most important Project. Be sure and focus on your Activity and Person of the Moment when you do it.

In my case, Kelly and I ended up following this PATH. For Kelly, the Harvest was attending a school she really loved with a top ten football team. She also earned a highly regarded degree that served her well in becoming a CPA and building her career.

Because she took the SAT preparation classes for testing, her already high scores went up over 100 points. She earned meaningful scholarship money that resulted in me harvesting tens of thousands of dollars in savings. That would not have happened if we hadn't done a PATH. My PATH took about ten minutes to do. You can do some very powerful thinking, very quickly, if you have a process. Remember,

PATH enables you to sort to…

…your most important Activity to move forward on

…your most important Project to accomplish

…your Achievement and Enjoyment goals in any quadrant.

When you are considering a project in any of your life quadrants, or if you are facing some uncertainty or dissatisfaction in your life, make a PATH. If you are building a home, refinancing a mortgage, shopping for a car, or planning a family reunion, make a PATH. You'll get it done more quickly, easily, and more completely. If you make a PATH for the next gathering you have in your home, it could allow you to actually relax and enjoy your friends instead of running around at the last-minute salvaging things that fell through the cracks. Making a PATH is not a fancy, formalized process. It is as simple as getting out a piece of paper.

Brian Stuart is an executive with a large regional bank. In addition to being a client, Brian is also a good friend. When he moved from Miami to Atlanta, he got out a pad and used PATH to plan the move. The move was the Project. He listed and prioritized the necessary (A) Activities. He took some of the activities, his wife, Ashley, took others, and they checked them off as they went. Brian, who had made several other moves, called afterwards to say it was by far the simplest and easiest relocation they had ever made. Making his PATH took him less than fifteen minutes. You can generate your own bountiful harvest in a similar time.

To see what I mean, take a few minutes now to create a PATH toward greater Achievement and Enjoyment with your family or friends using the worksheets in the following chapters or download and print the PATH worksheets here: worklifebalance.com/worksheets.

Summary

- PATH helps determine the most important projects and activities that will turn your Achievement and Enjoyment goals into reality.
- First, list out all of your potential Projects and prioritize them.
- Then, pick your most important project, identify all of the Activities required to complete it, and put them in priority order.
- Finally, WIN with a Time to do each activity and be sure to Harvest the benefits.

A PATH to Success With Family & Friends

"For of all sad words of tongue or pen, the saddest of these: It might have been."
— John Greenleaf Whittier

Now it is your turn to take ten to fifteen minutes to determine the most important Project to move you forward on your Achievement and Enjoyment goals with Family or Friends. I encourage you to do this exercise *right now*.

With your goal in focus, follow the four simple PATH steps below.

The PATH Method

P = Project	Using List and Prioritize, select the Project
A = Activities	Using List and Prioritize, determine the Activities to complete it
T = Time	Pick a Time for your A1 Activity and WIN
H = Harvest	Complete the Activity and Harvest the benefits

Follow the instructions through and WIN in your calendar with a specific Activity.

You will be delighted with your immediate Harvest on this project. You are now starting a PATH planning habit that will consistently make the things you want from life happen. Most importantly, you will be creating an even more successful Big Picture for yourself and those around you.

Use the PATH worksheets on the following pages or download and print free PATH worksheets for your individual use at worklifebalance. com/worksheets.

(P) - Projects
List & Prioritize (6-8 Minutes)

1. Circle either the Family or Friends section of your Big Picture as your PATH focus.
2. List <u>Project</u> options to Achieve & Enjoy more in that quadrant.
3. Prioritize each option as an A, B, or C.
4. Prioritize each A option as A1, A2, A3, etc.

Circle One: Family or Friends
(P) - <u>Projects</u>

Rank	Projects	Start Time
_____	_____	_____
_____	_____	_____
_____	_____	_____
_____	_____	_____
_____	_____	_____
_____	_____	_____
_____	_____	_____
_____	_____	_____
_____	_____	_____
_____	_____	_____

Transfer your A1 Project to the top of the Activities page that follows

(A) <u>Activities</u>
List & Prioritize (6-8 Minutes)

1. Write your A1 project at the top of the page that follows and list Activity options for implementing it.

2. Prioritize each Activity options as an A, B, or C.

3. Prioritize each A Activity as A1, A2, A3, etc.

4. Choose a specific time to do your A1 Activity and WIN (Write It Now) in your calendar on the day you will begin it.

Family or Friends PATH
(A) - <u>Activities</u> List & Prioritize

A1 Project - _____

Rank	Activities	Start Time
____	_____	_____
____	_____	_____
____	_____	_____
____	_____	_____
____	_____	_____
____	_____	_____
____	_____	_____
____	_____	_____
____	_____	_____
____	_____	_____

WIN!

(T) – Time
WIN with your A Activities in Your Calendar!

If you have taken the time to complete your PATH, congratulations. Now WIN with at least your A1 activity in your calendar. Your A1 Activity is your *most important* Activity to move you forward on your most important Project to accomplish your most important goals. It all starts with A1! Set a point in time when you are going to do it. If you do not WIN, then your PATH was probably wasted time and effort.

Continue now to WIN in your calendar with as many of the other A Activities as possible, recognizing that for some items you may not be able to select a time until you complete an earlier task.

When you WIN, you are literally assembling your future Big Picture and planning to make it happen. You become the designer and builder of your own life.

Summary

- You are now starting a PATH planning habit that will consistently make the things you want from life happen, creating an even more successful Big Picture.
- When you do a PATH, be sure you WIN to ensure you follow through.
- What would contribute to your Achievement & Enjoyment goals with your family and friends? Try creating a PATH for it now.

14

A PATH to Success
In Your Work

"By failing to prepare, you are preparing to fail."
— Benjamin Franklin

PATH is an especially powerful tool for Achieving and Enjoying more at work. Sherri owned a small accounting firm and had crafted this goal for herself:

Double my real net worth between now and age fifty-five by honestly building a firm that delivers good value to our clients and helps the development of all who work in it. Enjoy seeing the professional growth of employees and building relationships with clients. After 55, turn day-to-day leadership over to someone else.

Her Project page for an initial PATH towards achieving that goal looked like this:

Rank	Projects
B	Develop a new sales/marketing plan
B	Upgrade computer software
A3	Get Johnson proposal out
A2	Get more Play time with clients – build relationships
A1	Delegate more responsibility to others

Sherri wanted her top Project to be more play time with clients to build relationships, hopefully expanding referrals and new business. However, that had to be her A2 priority as she was too busy actually doing the clients' accounting work to have any time for socializing and lead generation. Before she could spend time with her clients and grow the business, she realized she needed to delegate more of her day-to-day accounting responsibilities. As a result, "Delegating" became her A1 Project.

The Project part of Sherri's PATH was completed. It took her about six minutes to conclude that her most important Project to achieve her goals in the work quadrant was to "Delegate more responsibility to others." She then moved on to the A step in PATH. The purpose of ranking our Activities is to prioritize what will help you achieve success in your Project and in what order. In Sherri's case her Activities prioritization and her Time scheduling looked like this:

(T) Time
A-1 Project (Work Quadrant) – Delegate more responsibility to others

Rank	Activities	Start Time
C	Hire new personnel	Set time to revisit next month
A2	Each team member makes PATH on their clients	Assign 9:00 a.m. Monday; back from others by Thursday
A1	Assign client coordination roles to others	9:00 a.m. Monday
A3	Have first weekly meetings for updates	9:00 a.m. Friday
B	Inform clients of new system	Set time next month

Sherri recorded each of the activity Times as WINs in her calendar and started with her team on this PATH at a 9:00 a.m. meeting she called for Monday. All of her employees had been trained on PATH, so they understood what was expected and were able to work quickly with Sherri on all of the Activities.

For Sherri and her firm, the Harvesting included an immediate increase in productivity for the entire company. Prior to making her PATH, Sherri had been the coordinator on all client projects. Nothing could get processed and out to the client without her seeing it. As soon as she implemented the delegation Activities, the bottle neck was cleared up and she had more time for other priorities. A manager on her team later told me that not only did everyone's effectiveness go up, but so did their job satisfaction because their client work wasn't always "Waiting on Sherri." The payback for Sherri, her coworkers, and her clients was almost instantaneous.

As a result, Sherri was able to move on to her A2 project shortly thereafter, "Get more Play time with clients." Instead of just doing clients' accounting work, she was able to develop relationships with them that resulted in more business and referrals.

Approximately two years after our initial contact with Sherri and her associates, she called to say that she had sold her firm and was moving to California. She was taking over as chief financial officer for one of her clients. She was financially well ahead on her lifetime work goal because of the sale. She no longer was heading day-to-day operations, which was one of her lifetime work goals. And her employees, who had participated in the buy-out of the firm, were very pleased. Sherri's Harvest was abundant.

Sherri and her team had done many things to make their organization successful. But a very important beginning step was that twelve-minute investment on Sherri's part to make a PATH. You can do some very powerful planning, very quickly, with this supercharged thinking process.

Now, Sherri was the sole owner of her business. As a result, she had a great deal of responsibility and authority to call the shots as she saw them. On the other hand, another example comes from John, someone who had almost no authority and limited responsibilities in his company.

John worked on the loading dock of a firm that built, stored, and shipped custom exhibits for trade shows. Their client list was blue chip. John assisted in pulling together the various components of an exhibit, packing, and shipping them. John began a PATH in his work quadrant by listing and prioritizing his **Projects (P)** as follows.

(P) Projects List & Prioritize
Work Quadrant

Rank	Projects
A2	Prepare Coke booth to ship
A1	Improve carpet inventory system
C	Redo my time-tracking sheets
B	Evaluate new rack purchase

Each unique exhibit that John shipped had custom carpet that went with the display. Because their carpet inventory system was in disarray, some exhibits were shipped without the carpet so they could meet tight deadlines. Once found, the matching carpet often had to be air-freighted from the east coast to Los Angeles, Chicago, or Stockholm. Not only did this cause difficulties for their clients, but it was costing John's company big dollars in unnecessary air shipment charges. This is why John's A1 Project to achieve more at Work became, "Improve carpet inventory system."

John continued his PATH with the **Activities (A)** for his A1 Project as follows:

(A) Activities List & Prioritize
A-1 Project (Work Quadrant) – Improve carpet inventory system

Rank	Activities	Start Time
A2	Clean out obsolete inventory	Wednesday/Thursday after 4:00 p.m.
A3	Alphabetize racks by customer	Friday after 4:00 p.m.
A5	Relocate inventory to alphabetical location	Saturday morning
A1	Get approval to do	Monday 8:30 a.m.
A4	Get Jimmy's help Saturday	Ask Monday

Having very little authority at the time, and being a smart individual, John made his A1 to "Get approval to do." He took out his calendar and selected a **Time (T)** to WIN. On Monday morning, he wrote a reminder to cover the plan with his boss. On Wednesday and Thursday, after he knew the bulk of his regular shipping would be done, he entered, "Clean out obsolete inventory."

He put his A3, "Alphabetizing the racks," in his calendar to do Friday. Jimmy was the fork-lift driver, and John needed his help. He noted on Monday to ask Jimmy if he could help him move the carpets on Saturday, when there was no shipping occurring. John put his A5, the actual relocation of the inventory, down on Saturday.

When Monday arrived, John walked into his boss and said, "Bill, we really need to do something about this carpet inventory system." Bill looked up, frustrated, and said, "I know, I know. I'm going to get to it, but I'm just too swamped now to get started." John responded by saying, "Well I would like to volunteer to do it, and here is what I would like to do," handing Bill the PATH you see above.

How long do you think it took Bill to approve this Project?

In seconds, Bill had said, "Go to it." Almost everyone in the company was aware of the problem, including John's boss. They had all been caught in an "As Soon As" Trap, putting off something very important to handle more urgent, everyday fires. "As soon as we get caught up, I'll get to it." Plenty of people had gone to Bill and told him something needed to be done, and Bill had replied, "I know." John was the only one who not only came with the problem, but also came with the solution, a solution it took him less than fifteen minutes create a PATH for.

Two months later, I got a call from the president of this firm. He told me the new carpet inventory system John set up had already saved them thousands of dollars in air freight and would continue to do so every month. John's **Harvest (H)** was an instant cash bonus, more responsibility, and a promotion within the year. John continues to make PATHs on his important work projects and to positively impact his company and his career.

There is always a link between your Achievement and Enjoyment goals and keeping and excelling in your current job. However, in making your own work PATH, do not just think of your current job or the most pressing potential Projects in front of you. PATH should also help move your overall *life goals* forward. List longer-term-impact Projects that might also be important to Achieving and Enjoying more in life. These could include additional education, exploring your own business, improving your computer skills, or talking to your boss about getting exposure to a new area of the company. Such things may not come up as a current A priority but having them on your list lets you give them the mental hearing they deserve.

Why not take ten to fifteen minutes now to apply PATH and achieve and enjoy more in your Work Quadrant with the exercise below?

Use the PATH worksheets on the following pages or download and print free PATH worksheets for your individual use at worklifebalance. com/worksheets.

Work PATH

(P) - Projects
List and Prioritize

Rank	Projects	Start Time
_____	_____	_____
_____	_____	_____
_____	_____	_____
_____	_____	_____
_____	_____	_____
_____	_____	_____
_____	_____	_____
_____	_____	_____
_____	_____	_____
_____	_____	_____

Work PATH

(A) - <u>Activities</u> List & Prioritize

A1 Project - Work Quadrant _____

Rank	Activities	Start Time
_____	_____	_____
_____	_____	_____
_____	_____	_____
_____	_____	_____
_____	_____	_____
_____	_____	_____
_____	_____	_____
_____	_____	_____
_____	_____	_____
_____	_____	_____

WIN!

WIN with your A Activities in Your Calendar Now.

In today's world, the most valued contributors on and off the job are those who initiate action, not those who sit around waiting for the world to act on their behalf. The buzz phrase for this is: "Be proactive." To turn this phrase into more than a buzzword, make a PATH for the things you want in life. Always prepare your recommended solutions, indicating their priority and when you intend to do them before you "take them to market" or seek advice or approval.

Make your own PATHs to success not just for challenges but for opportunities, as well. The world is filled with those everyday opportunities. In fifteen minutes or less, you can be on your way to achieving and enjoying more in your life.

Summary

- PATH is an essential tool for Achieving and Enjoying more in life and in work.
- When considering PATH for Work, think about both long and short-term Projects to add to your list.
- What would you like to achieve over the next few months or years at your job and over your career lifetime? Create and complete your PATHs to get there.

15

Your Most Important Self Project

"How well you maintain your vehicle, and the kind of fuel you use, will determine the quality of your journey."
— Jim Bird

A Self Quadrant PATH

If you look closely at the Big Picture visual earlier in this book, you will see what appear to be roads separating and running through your four different quadrants. They call to mind the often-used and very relevant analogy of life as a journey. To go on a journey, you usually need a vehicle. What is your vehicle?

Have you ever flown to an out-of-the-way place on a small commuter airline in a tiny, puddle-jumper plane? I took such a flight to do some fishing on a small island in the Bahamas, landing on a dirt airstrip. When I was ready to leave the island, I went down to the "airport" to ask the multi-talented local cook, customs agent, and airstrip manager if I could get a plane ride back to the United States that same day. His response, in a delightful Bahamian accent was, "Certainly, man."

He shouted a command across the field. After a short time, another man began to tow a very questionable-looking, dust-covered airplane from the bushes. With one tire almost flat, the plane limped onto the field hauled by the attendant. He managed to get the dented relic to the fuel pumps, shouting back, "Does this take gasoline or kerosene?"

Is this the kind of plane you want to fly in? At best, it's going to be one of those white-knuckle flights that raises your stress level and potentially ruins your whole day. At worst, instead of soaring, you could crash and burn long before the flight is supposed to be over.

Each of us is taking a "life flight" every single day. You are already sitting in the vehicle that will take you on your journey. Your body is like the wings, flaps, and fuselage of the plane. Your mind serves as the control panel and your guidance system in life.

This vehicle you are sitting in can take you to great heights. It can transport you to exciting places and wonderful adventures. But, if you are not maintaining your equipment or you put in the wrong fuel, you are going to have some pretty rough flights.

Fueling up with lots of alcohol, drugs, fat, nicotine, or sugar will short-circuit your control panel and jam your wings and flaps. This risks tragedy. No self-management tools will work if your vehicle isn't ready to run. So, fuel up right.

You are likely already aware that numerous studies show that the right foods and aerobic exercise are essential to keeping your vehicle maintained and ready for a long-life flight. Whether you want to increase your energy levels, enjoyment, mental clarify, or to overcome stress or depression, aerobic exercise is one of the most effective tactics available to you. Researchers highly suggest a simple *everyday* walk for thirty to forty-five minutes, which for many can produce life-changing results.[8]

If you are already maintaining a good eating and exercise routine, congratulations. Keep it up. If not, consider making a PATH for yourself that involves a diet and exercise program. Once you've decided on your actions, record your weight and exercise results each day in your calendar. Act and track. As the old cliché says, "What gets measured, gets done."

Remember too that "rest is a weapon." Much of Robert Ludlum's famous novel, *The Bourne Identity*, is set in one of my favorite cities,

---

[8] Younger Next Year, Chris Crowley and Henry S. Lodge

Hong Kong. The climax builds to a duel-to-the-death encounter in this city between the good-guy American agent, Jason Bourne, and his evil adversary, Carlos the Jackal. Knowing they will meet within hours, the evil spy prepares by checking his weapons and visualizing the anguish he will bring to Bourne before killing him.

Bourne on the other hand, goes to sleep. His logic? "Rest is a weapon," significantly increasing alertness, energy, and the entire body and mind's ability to function. Ludlum's observation is backed up by increasing amounts of researched data.[9]

Some of these studies show that an extra thirty to forty-five minutes of sleep a night can increase your energy level by as much as 25 percent. Other research has shown that avoiding caffeine after three o'clock results in better and more energizing sleep.[10]

Just as rest is an ally, "fatigue will make cowards of us all."[11] If you would like to increase your physical, mental, or emotional energy, put rest on your side. Try going to bed 45 minutes earlier tonight and drinking decaffeinated drinks after lunch. Try this for a few days and consciously observe how you feel during your waking hours. These two simple steps can result in substantial improvements in your Achievement and Enjoyment and in your ability to improve your Self quadrant.

Of course, you will have other, non-health related Projects in your Self quadrant. For example, you may be considering learning a foreign language or how to play a musical instrument, or enrolling for additional education. Whatever your potential Self objectives for the coming year, list them all and then use PATH to see which one emerges as your A1 Priority. Just keep in mind that how well you maintain your vehicle, and the kind of fuel you use, will be a major determinant of the quality and the length of your journey.

---

[9] Harvard Medical School, Division of Sleep Medicine

[10] Sleep Disorders and Research Center, Henry Ford Hospital, Detroit, MI and Department of Psychiatry and Behavioral Neurosciences, Wayne State College of Medicine, Detroit, MI

[11] Quote by Vince Lombardi

OK, now is the time to take ten minutes just for you. Make a Self PATH and WIN with it now.

Use the PATH worksheets on the following pages or download and print free PATH worksheets for your individual use at worklifebalance. com/worksheets.

Self PATH

(P) - <u>Projects</u> List & Prioritize

Rank	Projects	Start Time
_____	_____	_____
_____	_____	_____
_____	_____	_____
_____	_____	_____
_____	_____	_____
_____	_____	_____
_____	_____	_____
_____	_____	_____
_____	_____	_____
_____	_____	_____

Self PATH

(A) - Activities List & Prioritize

A1 Project - _____

Rank	Activities	Start Time
____	_____	____
____	_____	____
____	_____	____
____	_____	____
____	_____	____
____	_____	____
____	_____	____
____	_____	____
____	_____	____
____	_____	____

WIN!

Summary

- You are already sitting in the vehicle that will take you on your life's journey.
- How well you maintain your body, and the kind of fuel you use, is a major determinant of the quality and the length of your life.
- Regularly evaluate your Self goals, including for your physical and mental health, and make a PATH to achieve them.
- When you do, you are helping not just yourself, but also those who love and depend on you.

16

A Lifetime of Successful PATHs

*"Action may not bring happiness but there is no
happiness without action."*
William James

Now that you've learned PATH (and hopefully created a few of your own), I want to share three tips to make PATH an even more effective and positive habit in your life.

Use PATH, WIN, A.M. & P.M. and Happiness Meter Together

Illustrated below is the simple but powerful flow for PATH. Reinforce it by reading through this and mentally move around the circle, recalling what you have just learned in the prior chapters.

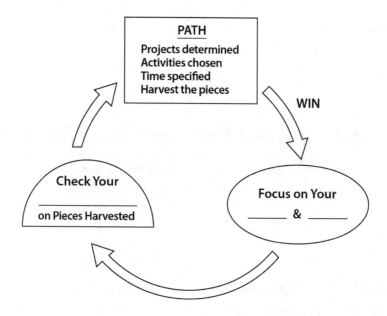

To make your PATH decisions a reality, you need to WIN with your choices. Then, to get the most out of those choices, you should focus on your Activity of the Moment and Person of the Moment as you implement them. Afterwards, check in with how you feel about the results (by using your Happiness Meter)

As you may have observed, the only significant difference between the TAP and the PATH Process is that

- TAP deals with People
- PATH deals with Projects

All of the other tools in the process remain the same.

Keep Your PATHs Visible

In making a PATH to determine and complete your next top project you create a valuable document that can change your future for the better, perhaps dramatically. You should keep that document readily accessible so you can quickly refer to the next Activity that you need to WIN with to move your Project forward. You have several options to do this. You can keep it on a notepad, on a loose page on your desk, or on your computer or phone.

By having your top project PATH readily accessible, you can avoid deferring to unimportant C priorities that land on your desk or in your e-mail unexpectedly. Instead, you can quickly flip to and focus on your next activity for your top project. You will be able to complete some of those A activities more quickly than many of your Cs. The difference will be that completing those As, will bring you much more satisfaction and real-life rewards. They will make your Big Picture look more like the one you have defined for yourself.

Make a Monthly PATH - Stay in Focus on the Most Important

Setting a monthly reminder to revisit your existing PATH and creating a new ones will keep you focused on your life's most important projects. Here's how:

1. Projects – At the beginning of each month, list and prioritize the Projects that are most important (not just immediate) to your Achievement and Enjoyment goals.

2. Activities – Create a PATH page to prioritize the Activities for at least your A1 Project for the upcoming month.

3. Time – WIN by setting time on your calendar for as many initial Activities as you can schedule.

4. Check In – Set a calendar reminder to check on your PATH status at least weekly.

5. Harvest – After completing an activity for your A-1 Project, congratulate yourself. You have done the most important Activity on the most important Project in your life.

Do this PATH once a month and at the end of a year you will have completed the 10 to 12 most important Projects in your life. This is more than most people accomplish in a decade!

In following through on your PATH, don't forget the Enjoyment side of your goals. Sometimes it's easy to get caught up in the completion of a Project and forget its original purpose. This happened to me at a birthday party I had planned for my father. It was a special affair with most of our family and close friends planning to attend.

The party was to be at my father's house. I had arrived early to make sure everything would go well. My Dad lived on a beautiful lake with a 15-acre pasture, so I had planned for the food to be served outside. I situated each table for a good view. I was making sure everything was just right. Then my father came down to check things out.

He didn't like the table arrangement. He started moving the chairs around because he thought it would be nice to be closer to the pool. I tried to explain to him why each of his moves wouldn't work well, but he didn't want to hear it. Before I knew it, we were arguing, duking it out with words, *on his birthday.* Fortunately, my mother was there and she quickly redirected our thoughts and efforts to something more productive. I immediately realized how foolish I had been.

I had forgotten the whole purpose of the effort. It was to celebrate my father's birthday, be together with friends and loved ones, and create a wonderful memory for my dad. Instead, I was arguing with him over table arrangements. Thanks to my mother we quickly made up. I focused on what the guest of honor wanted and we had a very positive outcome.

Remember the goal in life is to Achieve *and* Enjoy every day.

Summary

- Using PATH with WIN, A.M. & P.M., and your Happiness Meter will create an even bigger, positive impact on your life and Projects.
- Keep your PATHs visible to help you stay in focus and avoid unimportant tasks.
- Set a calendar reminder to revisit your PATH monthly.
- Set a new PATH once a month and you will complete up to 12 of your most important Projects in a year.

PART FOUR

Your Big Picture

Way of Life Goals

Tool #9

"It is the very activity of living a good life that is an end in itself."
— Aristotle

To achieve Aristotle's end of living a "good life," you must first define for yourself what a good life" is. This is the purpose of *Way of Life Goals*, the final tool in this book. Way of Life Goals bring clarity to what a "good," fulfilling life means to you. They let you see the front of the puzzle box—your Big Picture—clearly.

When audiences at our seminars are asked to name the goals they are pursuing, typical responses include:

- *Good health*
- *Promotion*
- *New home*
- *Self-employment*

- *Financial security*
- *New car*
- *Vacation*
- *Getting married*

Most goal-setting advocates would say that these goals are too vague to be successfully accomplished. These experts would tell you, "To achieve a goal, you need to be specific about what it is, when you want it, and how you are going to obtain it." Restated in these specifics, some of the above goals might look like this:

- *Maintain my weight below 165 and LDL cholesterol below 110 for the next three months by exercising at least three times/week and increasing fiber-rich fruits and vegetables in my diet.*
- *Be promoted to head of my area by January 31 by exceeding all my current project objectives and learning and exhibiting management and leadership skills.*
- *Have the down payment saved for a home design, similar to the picture on my refrigerator, by December 1 of next year by adding 20% of my gross paycheck to savings each month.*

This specific, defined approach is very valuable and important. However, if this is the only approach you use to goal setting, you will probably miss your most meaningful goals of all. That is because such specific goals don't define what a "good life" is for you over your lifetime. They are far too narrow and short-term to be called Way of Life Goals. Instead, specific objectives like those above are better thought of as Project Goals, which PATH will help you define and implement.

The Crucial Difference Between Project Goals and Way of Life Goals

So, what exactly is a project? And how do projects relate to Way of Life Goals?

Project – A chosen _point_ or _points_ on your journey, arrived at by completing a series of related activities.

Each project is one destination on your journey of life; it is not its overall purpose or goal. You should resolutely pursue the right projects in life. However, completing projects, by themselves, will not produce a happy and fulfilling life.

You may have seen the poster that shows a pile of adult play things including a jukebox, boat, water skis, tennis rackets, and a sports car all overflowing onto other goodies with the caption, "He who has the most toys when he dies, wins." I bought that poster because it was so wrong it was funny. Completing projects and accumulating things alone will not make any of us a winner in life.

Way of Life Goal – A _way of living_ and set of long-term values that you work towards *every* day.

A Way of Life Goal is not a point on your journey; it is a way of living. Although you may not be 100 percent successful, you should be trying and expect to live your chosen *Way of Life Goals* every single day.

Likewise, Achievement is not a point or points on your journey that you reach and pass through; it is *a way of life*. No matter how successful you are, you will need to keep achieving in some form, for the remainder of your life.

Enjoyment is also not a point on your journey. At least, I hope it isn't. You don't want to live your life waiting for enjoyment to come only on the weekends or that vacation or next year or when you retire. Enjoyment should be a *way-of-life* goal every single day.

Way of Life Goals give meaning to every day and therefore meaning to your whole life.

By contrast, Projects are not something you try to live every day. Instead they are specific destinations points you choose because you expect them to add to your way of life.

Using these distinctions, give yourself two minutes to identify each statement on the following page as *primarily* a Project (P) or primarily a Way of Life Goal (G).

Project or Goal

Label

P or G

1. In the next three years increase my net worth by 50%   _____

2. Become and stay financially independent doing work I can be proud of   _____

3. Get my children through college   _____

4. Raise my children to live happy, productive lives so we can enjoyably tap into each other for the rest of our lives   _____

5. Make five face-to-face sales calls on new prospects each week for the next four weeks   _____

6. Build ongoing productive relationships with my customers by helping them achieve and enjoy success in their business   _____

7. Improve my fitness level so I can run a marathon   _____

8. Maintain my physical health so I can continue to enjoy my relationships and achievements   _____

9. Practice using the tools in this book until their use becomes part of my daily routine   _____

10. Assist my spouse in accomplishing his or her Way of Life Goals so our relationship stays viable and exciting   _____

1.P 2.G 3.P 4.G 5.P 6.G 7.P 8.G 9.P 10.G

As you check your answers, remember that a project is just a point or a series of related points. Once it is completed, it is over. It is not a way of life you are trying to live every day. That's why numbers 3 and 7 are projects even though they may take some time to complete. Numbers 4 and 8, by contrast, are Way of Life Goals because you direct your efforts towards them almost daily.

Keep these distinctions clear so that you do not include short-term projects when defining the Way of Life Goals you will pursue every day.

Answering the Big Question: Why?

Way of Life Goals require that you stand back from your Big Picture and ask "Why?" Why do you want a better income? Why do you want a new house, or a promotion, or to put your children through college? Why do you pursue any of these project-based objectives? *Why do you want to achieve the things you pursue so intently on a daily basis?*

Is it to be happy? To have a sense of fulfillment; a feeling of security and well-being; to take pride in who you are and what you do? From hearing the responses of thousands of people to this question, my guess is that many, if not all, of these things are important to you. They certainly are to me. These all reflect the joy of living, our yearning for Enjoyment in our lives on an ongoing daily basis.

But there is one more fundamental "Why?" to answer. Why do you need to *achieve* anything at all in life?

This part of our "Why" is practical. Without any achievement, we would not have jobs that deliver essential income. Without this income and personal efforts to achieve, we couldn't provide many of the basic necessities that allow us to strive for happy and healthy lives for ourselves and those we care for.

The reality of life is:

We must <u>achieve</u> in order to *live*.

But just as importantly:

We must <u>enjoy</u> in order to make the living and achieving worthwhile.

Achievement also brings its own sense of joy, including pride, satisfaction, a sense of well-being, security, control and self-esteem.

Never lose sight of this simple reality:

Achievement and Enjoyment are the two essential purposes of our journey.

I know this seems simple. But not remembering that we must also make an effort to enjoy our lives is one of the reasons why so many financially "successful people" are not happy, or not nearly as happy as they should be.

For most of us living in a developed nation we are rich compared to most of the world's population. The median per capita household annual income worldwide is about $2,920.[12] That means half the world lives on less. Most of our poorest citizens today live in many ways better than the kings and queens of Europe did in the past. Prior to the nineteenth century, not even the lords and ladies had electricity, gas heat, motorized transportation or indoor plumbing. Most of us in developed countries are rich today. We are all part of societies that have and are *achieving* great things that make us better off economically. Fortunately, the rest of the world's poverty rate is also declining.[13]

How to Avoid the "As Soon As" Traps

If all it took was money, 99 percent of the people you come in contact with every day should be overflowing with happiness. Instead, too many of us are caught in what we referred to earlier as the "As Soon As" Trap. "As soon as I get through with this project at work honey, I'll talk to you again, I promise."

---

[12] Gallup, December 16, 2013
[13] The World Bank, Poverty and Shared Prosperity 2016

Life does not work that way. There will always be another project, another desire, another dollar to make, another challenge you want or need to pursue. If you let it, the "As Soon As" Trap will keep you constantly frustrated for your entire life.

You are caught in the "As Soon As" Trap when you substitute the pursuit of projects for the Enjoyment of the journey. The pursuit of projects is necessary for your *Achievement.* Just as necessary to your success is *Enjoying* the journey. Let me repeat this key point.

You are caught in the "As Soon As" Trap when you substitute the pursuit of projects for the Enjoyment of the journey.

Project completion <u>and</u> enjoyment of the journey are necessary to a good and positively balanced life.

Way of Life Goals – The Wide-Angle View

We have identified Achievement and Enjoyment as *essential ways of life* common to us all. My work with clients over the years on these two concepts has shown some common Way of Life Goals that almost all of us share.

To lead a full life of Achievement and Enjoyment and to assist the other important individuals in my Big Picture in accomplishing their Way of Life Goals of Achievement and Enjoyment.

In this context, we all have similar way of life goals, but how we accomplish them will be very different. What projects and relationships we pursue to Achieve and Enjoy will vary greatly. The individual pieces of our pictures will often look very different, while for the most part our broad Big Picture views resemble each other.

Your Way of Life Goal of Achievement and Enjoyment can be broken down into four Big Picture Quadrant Goals as follows:

- A Way of Life Goal in the <u>Work Quadrant</u>
- A Way of Life Goal in the Family Quadrant
- A Way of Life Goal in the Friends & Community Quadrant.
- A Way of Life Goal in the Self Quadrant.

Each Quadrant Goal should include both Achievement and Enjoyment aspects. Let's clarify the key elements of each.

Please take two minutes now to identify the items on the following page as *primarily* an Achievement (A) or an Enjoyment (E).

Achievement or Enjoyment?

Label

<u>A or E</u>

1. Successfully maintaining my physical health through the rest of my life   _____

2. Deriving satisfaction from the benefits of good health and fitness   _____

3. Attaining financial independence   _____

4. Maintaining a comfortable level of material wealth   _____

5. Taking pride in my work and accomplishments   _____

6. Having fun making things happen with co-workers   _____

7. Raising healthy, productive children   _____

8. Taking pleasure in sharing the journey with family   _____

9. Enjoying a happy marriage   _____

10. Building a lasting relationship with my spouse   _____

11. Helping my friends to achieve and enjoy in life   _____

12. Sharing leisure time with friends   _____

13. Being satisfied and content with my life as a whole   _____

1.A 2.E 3.A 4.A 5.E 6.E 7.A 8.E 9.E 10.A 11.A 12.E 13.A/E

The Achievement & Enjoyment Standard for Every Goal

A complete and impactful Way of Life Goal will include both an Achievement and Enjoyment statement. To create such goals, we must be able to clearly focus on which is which. To help do that, let's review some of the phrases in the previous exercise to see how standing alone they are lacking, but combined they can create very meaningful Way of Life Goal statements.

In group discussions, there is often debate about several of these. Number 1, "Successfully maintaining my physical health through the rest of my life," is primarily Achievement. You may think you are going to enjoy it, but that is not necessarily true, is it? I have an acquaintance who enjoyed his running fifteen years ago. Today, he continues it, but his groans and complaints make it clear that he no longer recognizes much Enjoyment from it. Number 2, "Deriving satisfaction from the benefits of good health and fitness," however, is clearly Enjoyment. If you put 1 and 2 together, you would have something like: *Successfully maintain my physical health through the rest of my life so I can derive the satisfaction, sense of well-being, and many other benefits of good health and fitness.*

This brief paragraph combines an Achievement statement with an Enjoyment statement, thus forming a Way of Life Goal. In this particular case the Goal would be for the Self Quadrant. The enjoyment element encourages celebrating and patting yourself on the back for the achievement of exercising.

Number 7, "Raising healthy, productive children," is an Achievement, although many people assume they will enjoy it. Assuming will not make it so. There are countless cases of parents who successfully pushed their kids to get the best grades, excel athletically, get into a good college, and get a good job, only to have them leave home and never want to speak to their parents again. Number 8 is, however, Enjoyment and combining the two would produce the following Way of Life Goal statement: *Raise healthy, productive children so we can take pleasure, pride and satisfaction in enjoying the journey of life together.*

Number 10, "Building a lasting relationship with my spouse," is definitely an Achievement. It is also one of those things you might assume you are going to enjoy, but that's certainly not guaranteed. Have you ever heard of anyone who stayed married for a lifetime but was miserable for most of the relationship? Combining Number 9 and 10 creates a Way of Life Goal that can keep you explicitly focused on both the Achievement and Enjoyment aspects of the relationship: *Build a lasting, loving relationship with my spouse so we can enjoy a happy and fulfilling marriage together.*

Explicitly stating these aspects of your relationship with your spouse will focus both of you on catching negative trends early. When you start to get on each other's nerves, or argue over petty things you will say, "Wait a minute. Our goal here is not just to stay together but to stay *happy* together. Let's do something about the way we pay attention to each other." One of the biggest reasons that many marriages are not happier is that Enjoyment in the marriage is not an explicitly stated goal for both spouses.

Answering the Big Question – Why?

Creating Achievement and Enjoyment Goals in each quadrant enables you to answer the big question we pondered earlier...*why?* Why do I get up in the morning? Why do I continue in this relationship? Why do I do anything at all? When the *why* is clear to you in each quadrant of your life, it is much easier to determine which life choices will help you put together the Big Picture you want, and which ones won't. Way of Life Goals are also easy for you to create, as you will see in the next chapter.

Reader's Note

In the following three chapters, you will have the opportunity to set your own Way of Life Goals in each quadrant. Before choosing which quadrant you will start with, it is important to read the Way of Life Goal example in the first three pages of the next chapter. After that, you can set your Work goal in Chapter 18 or, if you prefer to start on another quadrant, skip ahead to one of the next two chapters.

Summary

- Way of Life Goals are a set of long-term values that you work towards *every* day.
- Your Way of Life Goals give meaning to every day and therefore meaning to your whole life. They answer the big question: "Why?"
- Create your own Way of Life goals for each quadrant, with both an Achievement and Enjoyment statement in each.
- Live these goals every day and you will live your best life, with few regrets.

18

A Way of Life Goal for Your Work

"A person without a goal is like a ship without a rudder, wandering aimlessly on the sea of life, arriving nowhere."
— Earl Nightingale

Being blindfolded would greatly frustrate any attempt to put a puzzle together. You don't want to cover your eyes to most of the pieces. Similarly, when you are putting your life picture together, trying to see and sort all the pieces in your head is nearly impossible. As referenced earlier, the average individual can hold only seven pieces of information in her working memory at a time.[14]

Because of this, the best way to create a Way of Life Goal is to lay out the possible pieces of your goal in front of you. You do that by writing down all of the possibilities. Then you can easily sort, eliminate where appropriate, and connect the pieces to create a meaningful *Way of Life Goal*.

Use this approach to set one Way of Life Goal at a time for each quadrant. As you do, keep in mind the overall goal for meaningful work-life balance: *To lead a full life of Achievement and Enjoyment and assist the other important individuals in my life in doing the same.*

The steps based on this foundation for work-life balance are very simple.

---

14 George A. Miller, "The Magical Number Seven, Plus or Minus Two: Some Limits on Our Capacity for Processing Information," *Psychological Review*, 1956, Princeton University's Department of Psychology.

1. Under "Rough Draft," write down the Achievements and Enjoyments you want in this area of your life. In this chapter, we are focused on the Work quadrant. Do this without any inhibitions. Remember, no one is looking over your shoulder. Get all of the pieces that pop into your head onto paper.
2. Under "Finished Version," put your rough draft pieces together into a completed goal statement.

Here is an actual client example of how this process works. Katie is the Director of Corporate Sales for a software firm. She stays actively connected to each quadrant of her Big Picture. Katie has told me that setting this work goal had an important ongoing effect on the value she gets not only from her work, but from her life as a whole.

Example: Work Quadrant Way of Life Goal

Rough Draft

Achievement Factors

> *Attain Solid Personal Income/Financial Security*
> *Have Flexibility (Allow time for other quadrants) – Not all consuming*
> *Add value to my organization*
> *Stay proficient in technology/Improve skills*
> *Utilize my background of skills*

Enjoyment Factors

> *Pride in career*
> *Earn the respect of my peers*
> *Stimulating environment*
> *Control over my hours*

Finished Version

Continue to improve my professional skills and knowledge base. Be an important part of adding value to my organization. Maintain stimulating job assignments that allow me flexibility and control of my hours. Build income security and take pride in my work while enjoying the respect of and positive relationships with co-workers and customers.

Look again at this finished goal. What are the Achievement factors you see? Pick out a couple. What are the Enjoyment factors or words in this goal?

Clearly both Achievement and Enjoyment are evident, a combination that gives this statement the value of a Way of Life Goal. Also notice the Big Picture nature of this work goal. Although it is not restricted to Katie's current job, it can apply to every one of her days at work there or elsewhere.

After clarifying her work goal (and again four years later), Katie told me that this exercise had a significant positive influence on how she chose to live her life. Prior to committing her goal to writing, she was bothered by a gnawing guilt both professionally and personally. She felt guilty about her work, because she was not the CEO of a major organization, something she had seen colleagues do and believed she had the potential to do herself. On the other hand, she regretted that she wasn't doing more things at home, like drying flowers and baking bread.

By crystallizing her Achievement and Enjoyment work goals in writing, she realized that the things she was feeling guilty about were not the things that she really wanted. Her priority was to have a rewarding career with good economic income that *also* provided her the flexibility she needed to enjoy and achieve important things with her husband and children.

"Why should I feel guilty about not achieving what wasn't my goal in the first place?"

She shouldn't, and you shouldn't either. But unless you are clear on your Way of Life Goals you, too, may be living the life you want to live, and not know it.

Katie regularly shares with others one of the key lessons she learned—that in setting your Way of Life Goals, there are things that you have to put on the back burner, maybe indefinitely. Prioritizing your life is going to happen by design or by default. Why not make those choices yourself, as part of clearly defining your goals?

Today a message on Katie's refrigerator reads: "Live your life by design and not default." That is invaluable advice that setting Way of Life Goals helps you put into practice.

In implementing these steps for yourself, think out over your lifetime. If that seems too vast for you, think ahead for at least the next fifteen to twenty years. Focus on the broad Achievement and Enjoyment factors you want to experience every work day, whether you are in your current job or a different role or organization in the future.

To illustrate this long-term approach, here is another example from a client who worked in the health care field. He liked his field and pictured himself staying in the profession. His exercise looked like this.

Example: Work Quadrant Way of Life Goal

Rough Draft

Achievement Factors
> *Add to the quality of life*
> *Save lives*
> *Be a contributor*
> *Gain Personal Income/Security*
> *Improve skills*

Enjoyment Factors

Take pride in work

Have positive interactions with others on staff

Have Enjoyment and respect of peers

Finished Version

Achieve continued improvement of my skills in the health care field. Contribute to delivering life-improving, life-saving, life-extending services. Through this build income, take pride in my work, and earn the respect and confidence of staff and patients. Enjoy my daily interactions with everyone at the hospital.

This individual looked ahead and decided he wanted to stay in the healthcare field, at least as far ahead as he could see. But many of his Achievement and Enjoyment objectives at work could apply to a variety of positions or organizations in the future. As a result, his finished version reflects a "way of life" he can direct his journey towards every day, even as his current situation evolves.

Do not think too narrowly about your current role or job. Your Way of Life Goal at work should not include installing the new software, or hitting your quarterly quota, or getting a promotion. These are all projects. They are important, but they are not Way of Life Goals. Do think about the profession you are in now, as well as any different ways of earning a living that you might aspire to in the future.

As you create your own Way of Life Goal for the work quadrant, don't overlap into the other quadrants. A work goal should not be, "Make a lot of money so I can enjoy spending it on my family." You'll get to your family goal in a few minutes. Right now, focus on Achievements and Enjoyments in the professional part of your Big Picture only.

Now use the next page (or a separate sheet of paper) and give yourself three to five minutes to do the following:

1. Write down under "Rough Draft" the Achievements and Enjoyments you want in the Work Quadrant of your life.

Then take up to five to eight more minutes to:

2. Put your rough draft pieces together under "Finished Version" into a way of life goal statement.

Use the examples as a reference. Don't hesitate to plagiarize a little. I modify my Big Picture goals often from the good input I receive from clients. But don't forget, this is *your* work goal, not mine, or your boss's, or anyone's but yours. Don't over analyze. Trust yourself. Just start writing now and see what happens.

Use the Way of Life Goals worksheets on the following pages or download and print free Way of Life Goals worksheets for your individual use at worklifebalance.com/worksheets.

My Work Quadrant Way of Life Goal

Rough Draft

Achievement Factors

_____

_____

_____

_____

_____

Enjoyment Factors

_____

_____

_____

_____

Finished Version

_____

_____

_____

_____

If you have gotten to a fairly finished version of your work goal, congratulations! Look back over your finished goal. Do you clearly have both Achievement and Enjoyment factors in the goal? Do not assume the Enjoyment will automatically come with the Achievements. It is amazing how the Enjoyment fades away over the years if it is not specifically in your mind as a goal. So, include an explicit Enjoyment statement that identifies what you want to enjoy while you are achieving. The best way to be sure you have done this is to work the word "enjoy" into your goal. Do that now if it's not already clear. Also check to see that you did not include short-term projects or mix family, friends, or self outcomes into this Work goal.

Way of Life Goals give us a solid foundation on which to make our day-to-day decisions. Happy, well-balanced individuals have solid internal foundations as a result of clear goals, making it much easier for them to deal with a shifting external environment.

If you created a fairly finished work goal, hang it up in a place where you will see it often. Use it as a frame of reference in applying your talents and skills, as well as the tools and concepts you find valuable in this book.

If you struggled or hesitated in setting this quadrant goal, focus on the words Achievement and Enjoyment. Holding these two concepts alone in the forefront of your mind as *every day* goals will add great value and meaning to the rest of your life.

In our workshops around the world they have evolved into a powerfully meaningful and attainable re-definition of work-life balance. That definition from the first chapter is a way of life goal in itself!

Meaningful <u>Daily</u> Achievement *and* Enjoyment
in each of my four life quadrants: Work, Family, Friends and Self.

So, what is the answer to "Why do I get up in the morning? Why do I go to work? Why do I stay married?" It is so that you can achieve and enjoy something *every day* and help those who are important to you do the same. That, by itself, is a profound goal that brings positive value and balance, no matter who or what quadrant you are applying it to.

Summary

- To create a Way of Life goal, write down the Achievements and Enjoyments you want in this area of your life—without reservations!
- Next, prioritize the pieces that are most meaningful to you and use them to form a completed goal statement.
- Hang your goals in a place where you will see them often and use them to make day-to-day and life choices.
- Prioritizing your life is going to happen by design or by default. Why not make those choices yourself, as part of clearly defining your Way of Life goals?

19

A Way of Life Goal For Family & Friends

"Cherish your visions; cherish your ideals; cherish the music that stirs in your heart, the beauty that forms in your mind, the loveliness that drapes your purest thoughts; if you but remain true to them your world will at last be built."

— James Allen

Family and Friends

For most of us, our greatest joys and disappointments come from the Family and Friends quadrants of our lives. That is natural. The people we value the most usually fall into these quadrants and, as a result, our emotional ties here are the strongest.

We all want to build loving, meaningful relationships that we hope will last for the rest of our lives. Clarifying what you want the Family and Friendship relationships in your Big Picture to look like is a critical step in making this a reality.

I could give you hundreds of examples of wonderful Way of Life Goals in each of these areas. They've included statements like:

"Learn to love and nurture the unique individual that each of my children is becoming."

"Create one-on-one time with my wife to maintain and grow the special relationship we had before the children were born, so that when they leave home, we won't be strangers."

"Stay in touch with my closest friends, even though we may move apart, recognizing that with true friends, it is a matter of quality over quantity."

"Provide opportunities—through education, travel and exposure—for everyone in the family to learn and grow together and individually."

"Expand my friendships now that my family is smaller, being willing to risk the perils and heartbreaks to experience the adventure and joys."

"Be strong enough to discipline my child today so that she will not have to learn her lessons much more harshly from the real world, where excuses are not accepted."

Some of these lines are almost poetic. But you are not looking for Shakespeare here. You are looking for things that are meaningful to you.

All of these statements came from goals set in eight to twelve minutes. My personal examples that follow were originally set in a similar amount of time. It doesn't take long.

Review the following examples. Then pick either the Family quadrant or the Friends and Community quadrant and write out a Way of Life Goal for yourself.

Although it has undergone some modification, my Family Way of Life Goal has served me well for decades. Here's how it came together many years ago.

Example: Family Quadrant Way of Life Goal

Rough Draft

Achievement Factors

Be honest/open
Assist them in learning/achieving & enjoying life
Help them achieve & enjoy so I can achieve and enjoy more with them
Earn and show respect

Enjoyment Factors

Enjoy playing with them
Enjoy seeing them grow (Girls & Vikki)

As I did the rough draft, I was focused on my immediate family—my wife, Vikki, and my two daughters, Amanda and Kelly. In moving to my finished version, I recognized there were other important family members—my parents, my brothers and sisters, even to-be-created relationships that I wanted to be part of my lifetime family goal. As a result, my finished version looks like this:

Finished Version

"Regularly spend quality TAP time with each of my important family members to help them achieve and enjoy. Emphasize mutual honesty, courtesy, openness, and respect. To the extent that each of my family members is successful, our relationships will be filled with more Achievement, Enjoyment, and Love."

What Achievement factors do you see here? What Enjoyment factors?

Now look over the Friends & Community Quadrant example goal below for its Achievement and Enjoyment factors.

Example: Friends & Community Quadrant Way of Life Goal

Rough Draft

Achievement Factors

Help achieve—help in their careers
Have good common ground for communication
Be there when really needed

Enjoyment Factors

Emphasize play here
Enjoy time with other couples

Finished Version

"Spend limited but quality time with each of my closer friends (individuals and couples), with emphasis on Enjoyment, but being available to assist in Achievement objectives when possible and needed."

I have strong interest and commitments to my family and business, so my time with friends is limited. As a result, I have chosen to focus the time I do have with my friends on Enjoyment. This doesn't mean that I won't be there for a friend to assist in whatever way I can on serious issues, and I think that attitude is mutual with my closer friends. What it does mean is that my normal emphasis with friends will be on relaxing, laughing, and smiling rather than on overly weighty issues. You obviously will choose your own emphasis.

I was at the back of the room watching another facilitator conduct a training session when a young single man was going over his Family goal. He had written down for his Achievements: "To pursue the possibilities of getting married." As his Enjoyments he had written: "To enjoy the pursuit."

His goal was not only good for a laugh, it also provoked some meaningful thinking on the part of several individuals who were somewhat frustrated with their pursuit of potential partners. They seemed to recognize from his comment that they had been making this area of their life more a pressure-cooker chore than a positive adventure. They adjusted their goals and mindsets in positive ways due to this humorous, but relevant insight.

Now choose either the Family Quadrant or the Friends & Community Quadrant to set a goal. You may want to do only one of these goals now and come back to the other later, but you are welcome to do both. On the next page, give yourself three to five minutes to:

1. Write down under "Rough Draft" the Achievements and Enjoyments you want in the Family (or Friends & Community) Quadrant of your life.

Then take up to five more minutes to:

2. Put your rough draft pieces together under "Finished Version" into a working goal statement.

Use the Way of Life Goals worksheets on the following pages or download and print free Way of Life Goals worksheets for your individual use at worklifebalance.com/worksheets.

My Family Quadrant Way of Life Goal

Rough Draft

Achievement Factors

_____

_____

_____

_____

_____

Enjoyment Factors

_____

_____

_____

_____

_____

Finished Version

_____

_____

_____

_____

_____

My Friends & Community Quadrant Way of Life Goal

Rough Draft

Achievement Factors

_____

_____

_____

_____

_____

Enjoyment Factors

_____

_____

_____

_____

_____

Finished Version

_____

_____

_____

_____

_____

Look back over your goals for clear Achievement and Enjoyment factors. Don't assume either will occur to you automatically. "Helping my friends to achieve and enjoy in life" is an Achievement, but it is not a complete goal. I have clients say to me that this is an Enjoyment statement. It is not. You might assume you will enjoy helping your friends, but that is not necessarily true.

You can probably think of your own personal example similar to the one cited to me by a client named Carol. Her friend, Sue, was constantly calling her to dump her most current problems. Obliging her friend, Carol tried to help on each call. Isn't that what friends are for? However, Carol's efforts had gotten her to the point where every time the phone rang, she thought to herself, *Oh, I hope that's not Sue.* Because Carol, and probably Sue, had lost sight of the Enjoyment side of their relationship, it was losing its value.

Instead of letting a relationship continue to deteriorate, you can boost its value immediately by explicitly recognizing the two sides that give it value. "Sue, it's not that I don't want to listen to your challenges and help when I can, but sometimes let's just lighten up and focus on some fun stuff. And there are some pretty neat things happening with me right now that I wanted to tell you about." Part of being a friend is to help *both* of you achieve and enjoy.

At this point, you have hopefully set your Work Quadrant Way of Life Goal and have taken the opportunity to set your Family and/or Friendship & Community Goals, as well.

There is one important quadrant left to address.

Summary

- You may assume that enjoyment with friends and family will happen automatically, but over time we learn that it does not.
- When you make daily enjoyment a stated goal, and not just achievement, you will realize deeper, more valuable relationships.
- Take ten minutes to write an Achievement and Enjoyment goal for either your Family or Friends & Community quadrant now.

A Way of Life Goal for You

"To thine own self be true, and it must follow, as the night the day, thou canst not then be false to any man."
— William Shakespeare

Who's Left?

In today's fast-paced environment, the area of life that is most often overlooked is your self. You are too important to let that happen. By clearly identifying the Achievements and Enjoyments that make up your Self Way of Life Goal, you define an important part of who you are and who you want to become.

Take a few minutes now to clarify what you want to achieve and what you want to enjoy for yourself in life. To help you start, here is a representative client example.

Example: Self Quadrant Way of Life Goal

Rough Draft

Achievement Factors
Maintain health – weight and exercise
Stay mentally sharp
Learn & grow
Be physically & mentally healthy so I can achieve and enjoy fully

Enjoyment Factors

Pursue personal pleasures & hobbies
Spend time alone, fishing and reading
Add exciting new puzzle pieces

Finished Version

Stay mentally, physically, and spiritually healthy and active at least into my 80s, so I can enjoyably TAP into my life, continue to learn, grow, and enjoy personal pleasures. Take pride in meaningful Achievements during those years.

What Achievement factors do you see? What Enjoyment factors? Most of us share physical and mental well-being as part of our Way of Life Goals in the Self area. What are your objectives for yourself over a lifetime?

On the next page, give yourself three to five minutes to:

1. Write down under "Rough Draft" the Achievements and Enjoyments you want in the Self Quadrant of your life.

Then take up to five more minutes to:

2. Put your rough draft pieces together under "Finished Version" into a working goal statement.

My Self Quadrant Way of Life Goal

Rough Draft

Achievement Factors

_____

_____

_____

_____

_____

Enjoyment Factors

_____

_____

_____

_____

_____

Finished Version

_____

_____

_____

_____

I hope you took time to set a Self Quadrant goal. If you did, ask yourself if it was harder or easier than the others.

Overall, the self quadrant ranks as the hardest goal for most people to set. It is often challenging for us to think just about ourselves. In particular, we find it hard not to include family relationships or financial objectives. Often, we are concerned about being selfish in our goals.

By setting a Self Quadrant Goal, you are not being "selfish" in the traditional use of that word. Your family, friends, and work associates are very important to you. You have already set goals in these areas. But guess what? You also deserve to be part of your own Big Picture.

To connect well with your family, friends, and co-workers, you must be physically and mentally together yourself. Having a Way of Life Goal for your Self Quadrant is an important part of doing that, maybe the most important part.

Crystallizing each of the four quadrant goals keeps you from losing sight of enjoying the journey. These Way of Life Goals will keep you in focus not just on "What" you want to achieve but also "Why" you want to achieve it. The "Why" is what keeps you motivated over a lifetime.

When you get up in the morning, remember the importance of the simple goal: *"I want to achieve something today and I want to enjoy something today, and I want to help others achieve and enjoy today, too."*

Whether at work, with your family, with your friends, or with yourself, this alone is a very meaningful and successful way to live every day.

Summary

- You are too important to overlook creating your own Self goals.
- By clearly identifying the Achievements and Enjoyments you want to experience for your Self, you define an important part of who you are and who you want to become.
- Self goals also help you be more physically and mentally able, so you can better connect with family, friends, and co-workers.

You Can Change Your Big Picture

"Life isn't about finding yourself. Life is about creating yourself."
— George Bernard Shaw

Now that you have set your Big Picture goals, do not consider them permanently cast. Like all other major choices in life, you should periodically revisit your goals as you and your life picture grow and change.

All the choices you make have consequences and every day you are making thousands of them. Most of them are unconscious. This is because by not changing anything, you are choosing the status quo. Not changing things is a choice, one that can have critical consequences for you and others.

Most times, the status quo is a good choice. You have made short- and long-term commitments and assumed responsibilities. Your character, sense of self, and long-term happiness depend on how you choose to stick to those commitments. Your positive and negative impact on others will, too.

Because choosing the status quo can be such an important choice, it is valuable to periodically revisit your major life goals and overall direction, re-evaluating what you have chosen and why. This applies to both your Way of Life Goals and to the projects and relationships that you have chosen to pursue.

Occasionally, I will revisit my goals, projects, and relationships. I will get away from my regular life and take a little time alone to think through my Big Picture. I was on such a long weekend on a small island in the Florida Keys in my late twenties. I would get up early to do some fishing (one of the few things in life that motivates me to get up early). This particular morning, at 6:00 a.m., I found myself entering the small local grocery store on the island. I was there to have a sandwich made, so I could take it on the boat with me.

The only other customer in the store at that early hour had already ordered a sandwich and was waiting for it to be made. Unlike me, in my tattered fishing clothes, he was dressed in stylish shorts and a fashionable polo shirt. We struck up a pleasant conversation and I learned that he was a professor from Nebraska down for a week-long tennis camp by himself. He asked me what I was doing in the Keys.

My immediate response was, "I'm down here deciding whether I'm going to go back."

He looked puzzled. "What do you mean, go back?"

"Go back to my job. Go back to where I'm living. Go back to my relationships. Go back to my life. I occasionally take some time to evaluate my life and decide what, if anything major, needs changing."

"You don't really mean that," the professor said, sounding somewhat astonished. "You have to go back."

I smiled. "I don't have to go back. Usually I do, but not always to everything and everybody. And when I do go back, I know it's because I have chosen to."

"Oh no," his voice grew louder and tense. "You have to go back. You've got obligations. You can't just walk out on them. I have to go back, and you have to go back."

"No. I could choose to get on a fishing trawler leaving tomorrow for three months at sea and not tell anyone where I was going. If I did, that choice would have consequences for me and for others, but I could choose to do it."

I was startled by his increasing agitation. His face was flushed, his words loud, his tone resentful, confused. "I am the head of a department at a major university. I am married, with commitments to my family and my community, and I have to go back. I have no choice. I have to go back and so do you!"

I found myself backing away from him a little as I tried to calmingly say, "Don't misunderstand me, professor. I believe very strongly in sticking to my commitments. I am the president of a company with nearly a hundred employees and thousands of customers. I have the professional commitments that go along with that responsibility as well as extremely important personal relationships in my life. I would not irresponsibly abandon any of them. But I recognize that whether I return to all, most, or none of them, these are still my choices. And whichever direction I take, there will be consequences that I must live with."

"No! You can't pick and choose that way! I have to go back to my obligations and so do you."

"But you *are* choosing. You are choosing to go back. And most of the time I do go back, too, because the net positives of sticking to what I'm doing outweigh the positive and negative consequences of changing. But not always. This trip I am thinking through a current relationship to decide if it is in the best interest of both of us to continue long-term. And that relationship will probably change."

"No! No! No!" the professor said, head shaking, "I have to go back, and you have to go back!"

Further discussion only produced more frustration on his part. He was still shaking his head and saying, "You have to go back, you have to go back," as he took his sandwich and walked out of the store. He was adamant that he had no choice, and therefore, neither did I.

But I did, and so do you.

You can change your Big Picture.

Your future is a choice.

No object of choice belongs to the past.[15]

If we are to make good choices, obviously we must be very conscientious in weighing the consequences to ourselves and others. Good decisions do not put short-term pleasure over a lifetime of guilt, loss, or injury. Conversely, giving up long-term joy in order to avoid

---

[15] In the Nicomachean Ethics, Aristotle says, "No object of choice belongs to the past."

paying a short-term price in stress or anguish will not yield the best outcome for you over a lifetime.

Choice Does Not Require Change

On a particularly stressful day, a professional woman and very caring mom, wife, and friend—my wife Vikki—was asking herself "why" she did all this. She later told me that her frustrations were focused on the heavy demands that our daughters and I were putting on her. She was irritated, stressed, even angry. As she stewed on this, the "Keys Story" I related above came to her mind. A light bulb came on.

"I don't have to stay here! I can leave. I can pick up right now and not come back. I can choose." When she said that to herself, she immediately calmed down. She even laughed a little.

"Sure, I'm frustrated. After the last week, who wouldn't be? But I would never choose to give up the joy Amanda and Kelly bring me. My role and commitment as a mother is too important to me to ever suffer the consequences of choosing to give that up. I love my family deeply and they love me, and the joy that gives me far outweighs the stresses and pressures. I can choose to stay or go, and I choose to stay."

Vikki later told me that when she made that choice not to change things, the weight of her frustrations immediately lifted. Her load didn't seem so heavy. Recognizing she could choose *and was choosing*, immediately changed her whole attitude for the better. It did not eliminate the demands in her life, but it greatly reduced her frustrations and increased her happiness and satisfaction. She knew it was her choice.

To reference the title of an important book by one of history's great economists, Milton Friedman, we are all *free to choose*.[16] Use that freedom wisely.

---

[16] Milton Friedman, *Free to Choose: A Personal Statement*, 1990.

Summary

- It is valuable to periodically revisit your major life goals and overall direction, re-evaluating what you have chosen and why.
- Remember that by not changing anything, you are choosing the status quo. Not changing things is a choice.
- Revisit your life goals and make your ongoing life decisions a conscious choice—doing so can immediately change your whole attitude and future for the better!

Using the Tools Together

"If you can't describe what you are doing as a process, you don't know what you are doing."
— W. Edwards Deming

Let's do a quick review of the tools.

Tools at a Glance

TAP˚ – The Relationship Balancing Tool
> Think – Act – Play

PATH˚ – The Project Balancing Tool
> Projects Activities Time Harvest

WIN˚ – The Commitment Tool
> Write It Now in your calendar on the day you intend to do it

AM & PM˚ – The Focusing Tool
> AM = Activity of the Moment PM = Person of the Moment

The Happiness Meter˚ – The Emotional Awareness Tool
> Train your brain to live on the positive side

Date vs. Meeting – The Action and Play Tool
> Meeting: Action time with major decision topics
> Date: Play time with *no major decision topics* for any participants

Emphasis Settings – The Life Balancing Tool

Determine where to emphasize your efforts within and between your life quadrants

List and Prioritize – The Solutions Tool

Allows you to identify, see, sort, and arrive at reasoned solutions more quickly

Way of Life Goals – The Destiny Tool

Not a point on the journey, but a **way of living** every day

To lead a full life of Achievement and Enjoyment and assist the other individuals in each of my four life quadrants do the same.

To combine the impact of these tools, start by thinking of your life and goals in the four relationship areas you see pictured in the Big Picture: **Work, Family, Friends & Community, Self.** Pick a quadrant to focus on. All of your goals and objectives in your chosen quadrant are accomplished by managing primarily only two things—your relationships with **People** or your **Projects** and activities.

Your Big Picture

Friends & Community   Self

Family   Work

To help manage the People piece of your puzzle (your relationships), use **TAP** to identify what you should emphasize in the relationship—Thinking, Acting, or Playing. **PATH** allows you to do similar prioritizing and planning for you most important Projects and activities. Once you have sorted to your most important People or Project priority, you need to commit to it so it doesn't fall through the cracks. **WIN** is the commitment tool to use to make that happen.

At that point, you have identified your most important People or Project priority, you have created a plan to improve it, and you've committed that plan to your calendar. Now, you follow through to create your intended impact by focusing on your **AM & PM.** Concentrating on your Activity of the Moment and Person of the Moment helps you stay committed and engaged to ensure all of your efforts and all of your moments have the most positive desired effect.

Using the above tools together results in better relationships and more projects successfully completed.

Your **Happiness Meter** gives you feedback to stay in touch with your emotional status. Use this emotional feedback as a trigger to Think through the direction of your relationships and projects and maintain or adjust them accordingly.

Remember too that…

Work-Life Balance really means:

Meaningful *daily* Achievement and Enjoyment in each of your four life quadrants
Work – Family – Friends – and Yourself

…And to use these tools to escape the "As Soon As" Trap

These tools are not a straitjacket system that requires using all or none. Use the tools that work best for you. It is literally impossible not to have your achievement increase your achievement, enjoyment grow, and positive balance improve if you are applying one or more of them regularly. These tools and methods really do work.

To make these tools—and the many skills you already bring to the table—work even better for you, the next chapter's message is one you have probably heard talked about many times before. It is a lesson, however, that anyone, at any age, can benefit from and it is a vitally important addition to your Achievement and Enjoyment in life.

Making an Attitude Investment

"I will speak ill of no man and speak all the good I know of everybody."
— Benjamin Franklin

Daniel Goleman in his best-selling book, *Emotional Intelligence*, documents that a positive attitude and hope is a more accurate predictor of a person's success than his or her IQ or prior life successes. One of many studies he quotes was done with the incoming freshman class at the University of Pennsylvania. It showed that the students' scores on a test of optimism were a better predictor of whether they earned good grades during their freshman year than their SAT scores or high school GPA.[17]

On the opposite side of the attitude equation, Dr. Redford Williams' study that was previously mentioned showed a seven-fold increase in death rates by the age of fifty for doctors who scored the highest on hostility scores, as compared with those who scored the lowest.

In short, your attitude not only affects how well you live, but how long you live.

I was very fortunate, in my early twenties, to be exposed to and understand the importance of a positive, can-do attitude. One of the best summaries on the power of attitude is, "Life's attitude towards you is a reflection of your attitude towards life."[18] Life is like a mirror. If you smile at life, life tends to smile back. If you frown at life, then life is going to look back at you the same way.

---

[17] Martin Seligman, *Peter Shulman Study*
[18] Originally attributed to Earl Nightengale

You learn this very quickly in cold-call selling, which is where I began my career. If you go in frowning at a receptionist, she is going to frown right back at you. If you smile, she smiles.

The type of cold calling I was doing was face-to-face. I walked into an office to see someone without an appointment. At first, I approached the receptionist hesitantly, in a reticent, defeatist way saying, "Umm, I'm Jim Bird. Could I, ahhh, see Mr. Johnson?"

The predictable reflection that came back was a stern frown followed by a question, stated more as a demand, "Do you have an appointment?" The result was, of course, I earned almost no meetings or sales.

After much frustration, I learned to change the attitude of my approach. With a big smile on my face I would stride in, extend my hand to the receptionist, and say, "Hi. I'm Jim Bird. How are you today? Great. I'm here to see Mr. Johnson. Would you tell him I'm here?" Do you think my responses changed?

Absolutely. A very high percentage of the time I got a smile reflected back. Now sometimes they smiled and still said, "Do you have an appointment?" But much of the time they would ring their boss or go get him. I began to get my share of presentations. My sales skyrocketed and even though I had only recently graduated from college, I soon became one of the top producers in an organization of seasoned sales professionals.

What I have recognized since then is that each of us is selling all the time. Every day you are selling your ideas or approaches to your co-workers or boss. You are trying to sell your spouse or significant other on seeing the movie you want to see. You are trying to sell the kids on keeping their room cleaned up. Your attitude will have a major impact on your success with co-workers, clients, friends, family and yourself.

But what if you are not a natural smiler? How do you then get a smiling attitude inside that reflects right out through your face to others? Since I am not a natural smiler myself, I had to learn a way.

Since then in sales training I have taught thousands of individuals how to generate that smile on demand. And it is very easy.

When you are getting ready to walk into that important meeting with your boss, or to make that key presentation, when you are feeling uptight and stressed, pause before you walk in and just think of something that makes you happy.

It could be chocolate, or pizza, or someone you love. Do it now. Just mentally dwell on something you really enjoy for a couple of seconds. Feel a grin coming? Do this same thing before your next important meeting and you will walk in with a big smile on your face. I certainly did with all those receptionists.

Don't worry, they don't know what you are thinking.

Both the scientific studies and everyday life experiences consistently prove that:

Good Attitude = Good Results
Fair Attitude = Fair Results
Bad Attitude = Bad Results

And this is true in every quadrant of your Big Picture. It is true both when you are relating to people and when you are tackling a project. If you begin a project with the attitude that *I hate doing this and it's going to take forever to do*, then it probably will take what seems like forever, and your results will be disappointing. If you have the attitude that *I'm going to get it done and get it done well*, then you probably will.

Now, this is not to say that if you change your attitude, the facts of life will change. They will not. What the research clearly shows, however, is that a negative attitude, no matter how good your skills, stacks the odds against you in life. By contrast, a positive, upbeat attitude tremendously increases your odds for success and happiness.

Our attitudes are incredibly powerful. They can bring about marvelous Achievement and wonderful Enjoyment. Despite this fact, there are literally tens of millions of people waiting for the circumstances or people that surround them to change before they will change. And that doesn't work. I know. I tried it for years.

I'm a bit ashamed to admit how foolish I was in my very early twenties. I had consciously made a decision not to smile at anyone until they proved to me they deserved it. I actually did this with forethought. My attitude was, *I will not give you a smile until you prove to me you are worthy of it.* I still shake my head when I think about it.

Well, guess what happened? I never found out whether anyone was worthy of my smile. No one would give me the time of day.

Then I made a thirty-day investment that changed my life.

An Attitude Investment

I didn't need scientific studies to prove the value of my investment. I immediately experienced the benefits of investing in a positive attitude. What I have to remember, and we all have to recognize, is that to get a return from life, we first have to make an investment in life.

This is true in the financial world, in relationships at work, at home, and in your everyday dealings with all the people you encounter.

There is no gain unless you take some risks.

Sometimes you make an investment in a person and you lose. The receptionist may frown back at your smile. Sometimes you get a little payoff; she smiles back, but you still don't get in to see your intended prospect. And sometimes you get a big payoff. You get the sale, you make a best friend, you get the promotion, you have a breakthrough in your relationship with a loved one.

But I guarantee you, if you make no investment, if you take no emotional risks, there is no possibility of gain.

So, I propose to you that for the next thirty days you make an attitude investment that will change your life, at least a little and probably a lot. This is an investment that requires no outlay of time or money.

For the next 30 days, invest in every person you come in contact with.

Invest a smile, a friendly attitude, an interested tone, a question. Really listen to your spouse or roommate tonight when they are trying to talk to you. Fold up the paper and ask some questions about what they are saying.

In doing so, think of that person as the most important person in the entire world; and treat him or her accordingly. Think of that person as your favorite movie star or renown athlete or leader.

Do this with every single person you meet. You will be amazed at what happens.

Now, there are two reasons why you should treat the young man behind the counter at McDonald's with the same positive attitude you would treat your best friend or your boss or the leader of your organization.

First of all, to them, who is the most important person in the world? That's right, whether they clearly focus on it or not, they are.

Second, by making this investment in others you are forming a great habit that then pays off for you automatically. Because you get in the habit of treating everybody positively and with respect, you don't pick up the phone in a gruff mood and say, "Yeah, who is it!" and find the president of your company on the other end of the line.

So, for the next thirty days, treat every single person you meet as the most important individual in that moment. Go out of your way to smile and be friendly. When you are coming into work tomorrow, make eye contact in the parking lot with others walking in and smile and say "Hi." Do the same when you walk into the bank or grocery store. It's fun, and you will be extremely pleased with the real results produced by all these good reflections coming back to you.

On one of my many trips to Miami, I was at the airport and in a hurry to get a rental car. When I arrived at the counter, one other person had just arrived in front of me. I was relieved that there wasn't a long line and expected to have my car fairly quickly.

The guy in front of me turned out to be a time-management freak who had absolutely no respect for anyone else around him. When he got to the counter, he threw down a printed reservation form and gruffly demanded action. "Richards. There's my reservation. Get me my car quick!" He then looked away, focused on his phone.

The agent behind the counter attempted to ask him a question, "Sir, would you like an upgrade—"

He cut her off in mid-sentence. "Can't you read? I've reserved the best car you have. Just get me my car; I want to get out of here." He then returned to texting away. The agent politely attempted another question and received the same kind of rude, "Hurry up, I am an important person and you are a nobody," response.

Well, the agent slowed to an absolute crawl. She went from being a speed typist to a laggard hunt and pecker. "Oh, I'm sorry, sir, the computer has misprinted. We'll have to start over." It took him forever to get his car.

Now I do believe in trying to treat everybody well. However, this guy's holier-than-thou attitude had gotten to me. When he finally did leave, I was tempted to stick my foot out just in case he wanted to trip over it and fall down.

When I did get to the counter, I made it a point to smile at the agent. I noticed from her badge that she had a very pretty name and complimented her on it. She smiled and I said, "I hope most of your customers aren't like that last guy." She said, "No, we just get a couple of jerks like that a day." We had a very nice, but brief conversation as she rushed me right through.

I am a cost-effective traveler and to get a good rate I usually rent a modest car. Well, this delightful rental agent must have given me three upgrades at no charge. In fact, I think I got the other guy's car. There is no telling what she put him in.

In this small, everyday example, I got a better product in a shorter time, and had much more pleasure in doing it—simply by treating the woman on the other side of the counter to a smile, and the respect and dignity she deserved.

The world doesn't care whether you Achieve or Enjoy, and it doesn't care whether you are happy or sad, or whether you evolve as a person or not. That is your responsibility.

And to continually get from here, where we started:

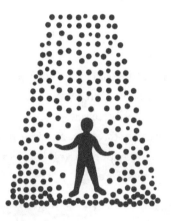

to here, where we all want to be:

we need to Think with a good process, and Act and Play with a good attitude...that strong, expectant, upbeat, lover of life attitude. It can really be that simple.

Summary

- To get a return from life, we first have to make an investment in life. This investment starts with your attitude.
- Your attitude not only affects how well you live, but also how long you live.
- Each of us is selling every day; attitude has a major impact on "selling yourself" successfully to co-workers, clients, friends, family and yourself.
- For the next thirty days, try an experiment. Invest a little something in every person you come in contact with and see what happens in return.

Getting the Most from This Book

"We are what we repeatedly do. Excellence then,
is not an act, but a habit."
— Aristotle

Here are four simple things you can do to double the lifetime benefits you get from this book.

Complete This One-Minute Exercise

Which of the following tools and concepts do you expect to be most meaningful to you on an ongoing basis? Take sixty seconds to circle your top three and commit to putting them into practice.

Summary of the Tools & Concepts

1. TAP	7. A Meeting vs. A Date
2. WIN	8. Attitude Investment
3. A.M. & P.M.	9. Emphasis Settings
4. The Happiness Meter	10. Achievement & Enjoyment
5. PATH	11. Way of Life Goals

6. The Big Picture
(Four quadrants)

12. List & Prioritize

Tell Somebody

Telling or teaching something to others is one of the best ways to retain it yourself. Pick three individuals now that you will explain the tools you circled on the previous page and WIN on the day you will do it.

Apply One of the Tools for All of Next Week

Earlier we discussed that Benjamin Franklin felt he owed all his success and happiness, all his Achievement and Enjoyment, to one thing: his method of improving his life and character. He would choose thirteen important areas to work on and then devote a week's strict attention to one of those things, leaving everything else to its normal chance. At the end of thirteen weeks, he would begin the process again.

Why not begin using Ben's proven method with the one tool or concept that you think will be of most value to you on an ongoing basis? Pick that one to fully focus on every day for the next week. If it's A.M. & P.M., set a daily A.M. & P.M. reminder in your calendar. If it's TAP or WIN or AM & PM, take thirty seconds now and write those reminders. By focusing on one thing, you will make more progress in a week towards mastering it than you otherwise would make in a year.

Review This Book Soon

One important thing you can do is to periodically look back over this book. Doing so will greatly multiply the ongoing value you receive from it. The most effective time to do your first review is at least one day, but no more than one week, after you finish the book. Pick a specific ten-to-twenty-minute period of quiet time. Use that time to look back over the tools, exercises, and your personal highlights. Why not WIN with your review time now?

I expect you will rewardingly and happily TAP into many more individuals on your journey and travel many more PATHs to success. You have the tools. They really do work.

You know that you have the ability. Now go out and apply those abilities and these tools with a great attitude. Make it happen for yourself, your colleagues, and the people you most care about. Every day, for the rest of your life,

Achieve and Enjoy.

Thank you for letting me, through this book, be part of your journey.

Work-Life Balance Resources

Redefining Work-Life Balance Online Workshop

If learning via video is your preference and you would like to take the Redefining Work-Life Balance course at your own pace, this workshop series leads you through the application of the tools to create immediate results in both your work and personal life. Upon completion of the workshop, you will have tools to create more achievement, enjoyment and positive balance for you and those you care for over a lifetime. Get the course at http://wlb-university.thinkific.com/.

Redefining Work-Life Balance Live Workshops

A workshop at your location is the next step to align your team around more productive achievement and more positive enjoyment on and off the job and instill a common language that excites and inspires your organization. Your outcomes will be measured increases in individual commitment, accountability and productivity, less negative stress, better teamwork and communication, improved morale, and increased trust and engagement levels. Discover more at WorkLifeBalance.com.

Redefining Work-Life Balance Train-The-Trainer

Do you want to teach your larger organization to achieve and enjoy more, be less stressed and more positively balanced every day on and off the job? If you want to increase and maintain high levels of discretionary effort and trust by providing your whole team with tools that create success, accomplishment and joy, on *and* off the job, we will train your facilitators. Learn more at WorkLifeBalance.com.

Redefining Work-Life Balance Keynotes

For keynotes by Jim Bird, the pioneer in work-life balance skills and results, contact us about availability for this tailored, upbeat, immediate impact one-to-two-hour interactive session. Your audience will walk away having already executed on key work-life balance decisions and retain take-aways that will add to their work and life achievement, enjoyment, and positive balance over a lifetime. For more information go to WorkLifeBalance.com.

Tula – The Work-Life Skills Dashboard

Tula can serve as your organization's ongoing Work-Life Balance skills resource for your entire team. It includes access to our online courses, work-life balance apps, one-minute solution worksheets, and new short read expert articles that supplement an initial library of work-life balance, stress management, time management, and leadership resources. To provide a valuable ongoing work-life skills resource for your entire team find out more at WorkLifeBalance.com.

WorkLifeBalance.com

Redefining Work-Life Balance for more Achievement and Enjoyment
for you and your organization

877-644-0064

CPSIA information can be obtained
at www.ICGtesting.com
Printed in the USA
BVHW041525280419
546749BV00010B/248/P

9 781948 787833